Turning Kids on to Print
Using Nonprint

Turning Kids on to Print Using Nonprint

James L. Thomas, Ed.D.
School of Library and Information Sciences
North Texas State University

Illustrations by Carol H. Thomas
and photographs by James L. Thomas

1978

Libraries Unlimited, Inc.
Littleton, Colorado

LIBRARIES UNLIMITED, INC.
P.O. Box 263
Littleton, Colorado 80160

Library of Congress Cataloging in Publication Data

Thomas, James L., 1945-
    Turning kids on to print using nonprint.

    Bibliography: p. 163
    Includes index.
    1. Audio-visual education.   I. Title.
LB1043.T49   371.33   78-9075

ISBN 0-87287-184-3

For my students—

past,

present, and

future.

TABLE OF CONTENTS

ACKNOWLEDGMENTS

The author wishes to thank those individuals who willingly gave of their time

Ruth Southard for her suggestions and guidance,

Judith Miller for gathering the current costs of the nonprint items,

Doris Laing for typing the manuscript,

and

Carol Thomas for drawing the illustrations.

INTRODUCTION

Much has been written on the problems children and young adults are having in the area of reading. All one has to do to discover the sad reality of this all too prevalent problem is to examine the local newspapers at the end of each year when the reading tests are given and the results are displayed. The findings usually reveal that most youngsters are reading at least one or two levels below their grade expectancy.

Numerous programs have been tried, tested and validated to improve or bring up the reading levels of our youngsters: some with success and some with little success. Millions of dollars are invested each year by publishers to develop the best basal reader that will provide the sequential skills necessary for the child to learn to read from kindergarten through senior high school. Supplemental texts are also written to help the child with specific skill deficiencies to increase his or her mastery of those skills in order to then proceed with the prescribed program.

Another reality that we as parents, teachers and librarians must come to grips with is that the youngster of today is surrounded by media in a variety of forms from print in hard and soft cover to nonprint through recordings, television, 8mm movies, filmstrips, and microforms, to name only a few. The question therefore needs to be asked: Which medium is most effective in reaching the child? If the kindergarten child comes to school after watching thousands of hours of cartoons, Sesame Street, Mister Rogers, Zoom, etc., to what degree can we expect that child to be ready to read? The youngster has been so conditioned by the realm of nonprint, of instant entertainment, of instant information, that to sit quietly and to listen to or read a story independently is not only difficult, but perhaps in some cases, impossible. If indeed we face these problems, and *face them we must*, then what alternative do we have to offer? What can we offer to those students that have experienced so much difficulty in learning to read that they are completely turned off by the process? What do we have for the average student that slips by and reads as little as possible, or for the bright student that gains his or her information by watching and listening to instructional materials or can plug into the computer for instant replay and feedback?

Numerous educational foundations have systematically investigated the problems surrounding children's mastery of reading. Most recently the Academy for Educational Development published their findings in *A Reason to Read: A Report on an International Symposium on the Promotion of the Reading Habit* (1976). Among the three practical problems this group chose to mention was "The Effects of Nonprint Media." Specifically, they pointed out that

> The influence of nonprint media on reading depends . . . on how they are used and what is expected of them. Although research is conducted regularly by major networks and government agencies on people's reactions to commercials and the emotional content of programs, little is known about the influence of media on reading motivation. The nonprint media now play a central, pervasive role in people's lives. How they can be combined with reading activity to be mutually reinforcing is one of our most compelling current research questions (p. 22).

Barber-Smith and Reilly in their article in *Audiovisual Instruction*, "Use Media to Motivate Reading" (December 1977), describe how learning-disabled students become more involved in social and academic activities through media productions. They point out that

> If students discover that they can improve their reading, even slightly, through participation in media productions, they may feel more motivated to read in other instances. If students experience some success in an academic area that was previously frustrating and discouraging, they are likely to feel an increase in self-esteem. This increase often translates into greater efforts in the classroom, both academically and socially (p. 34).

The approaches described in this book should in no way be misconstrued as the ultimate panacea for curing all reading illnesses. They are, however, offered as possible supplemental programs for involving students in instructional graphics production that has been found, through trial and error, to be highly successful.

Each chapter is systematically arranged for easy reading so that at a glance the reader can determine 1) the specific objectives of the process, 2) the strategies to be used in winning over the student, 3) the definition of any terms which the reader might not be familiar with, 4) the materials to be used and the maximum costs expected, 5) the exact step-by-step procedure to use in producing the item, 6) a sample format from an actual graphic produced by students, 7) suggested follow-up activities, 8) a bibliography with page references for further information, and 9) a list of possible suppliers of the equipment and software items used in each production.

TURNING KIDS ON TO PRINT

From my years of experience as a secondary and an elementary media librarian, I have become convinced that "tuned out" children can be "turned on" with media. While this in itself appears to be a worthy goal, I think that media is used to best advantage when it serves as a catalyst to return children willingly to the world of print.

While serving as librarian at a private military academy for high school aged boys, my background in English and speech made me the only candidate for teaching a course in public speaking. The post-graduates for whom the course had been planned were young men who had had academic difficulties throughout school and who were hoping to improve their grade record with an additional year of study. For six weeks I used the traditional approach to teaching speech: demonstration, textbook readings, speech assignments, and presentations. By the end of the six weeks, the students were as "turned off" as when they had entered the class.

In search of a new approach, I chose a number of projects involving media. Each student was assigned to write and tape a commercial on a product of his own choosing. Students were also asked to prepare a slide-tape presentation on a subject of particular interest. One football player enrolled in the class did his presentation on art history; another student, admired as one of the top wrestlers in the school, depicted the spiritual life of the youth of America.

Another project was a group effort culminating in a ten minute televised instructional program. To accomplish this goal, the students learned storyboarding, scripting, operation of the VTR and camera equipment, and how to involve others at the academy to help in their presentation. Their final projects took the form of 8mm films on such topics as wrestling and weightlifting.

Reprinted with permission from *Audiovisual Instruction* (September 1977).

The new approach had worked as I had hoped. The students became totally consumed by their assignments and even managed to spread their enthusiasm to other students and to the faculty as well. While nonprint media was used as a focal point, the students had to rely heavily on print in order to complete their projects. The use of media served as a source of motivation for a wider use of print.

I encountered a similar experience when I served as media librarian for a small rural elementary school. A fourth grade teacher approached me one day for help with a number of students she termed "reluctant readers." Their history of failures and a moderate amount of name calling by other students in the school had convinced them that they were at the "bottom of the heap."

Although I had never attempted to produce a filmstrip with such a young group, we decided to devote thirty minutes each day for a period of two weeks to such a project. The final product was to be shown to the Parent Teachers Organization. Students were organized into committees with responsibilities for art, script, layout, and filming. In addition, each child was responsible for the design and script for one frame. Students who had shown great reluctance to use books, encyclopedias, or even magazines, now devoured the printed page for information to be used in their filmstrip frame. The final product was both an individual and a group success. The recognition gained from other students and from the parents further reinforced the satisfactions that the students had gained from their research.

While much has been said and written about the advantages of using media with gifted or bright students, I believe it offers many benefits for the "turned off" or slower student as well. The use of media should be considered an avenue through which print can become more attractive and more meaningful to the student.

CHAPTER 1

STORYBOARDING: "THE 1, 2, 3 OF IT"

Frank Borman Elementary
Denton, Texas

CHAPTER 1

STORYBOARDING: "THE 1, 2, 3 OF IT"

INTRODUCTION

Anyone who has a background in teaching knows that a lesson does not have an obscure beginning, ramble from point to point, and end abruptly. If this were the case, students would more than likely be guessing their way through everything we attempted to teach. As a result of such disorganization, very little learning would probably take place. To keep our instruction clear and hopefully meaningful to others, normally it is necessary to organize it into steps with some logical progression. Step by step planning and presentation of this plan through instruction, if done correctly, is not easy, but is essential *if* our message is to be received and understood by our students.

A handbook such as this could be used a variety of ways: the most useful would be to read the one chapter of interest and read the others as time permitted; however, if this were done, one of the most important chapters might be omitted— storyboarding, which quite succinctly is "The 1, 2, 3 of it." The "it" simply means *all* of the processes which are to be described in chapters two through seven have as their origin a first step—and this is IT: storyboarding. Just as an instructional lesson must have a beginning, so must *all* of the nonprint production items covered in this book.

At the beginning of this chapter is a special notice: Read Storyboarding: "The 1, 2, 3 of It" FIRST. This means what it says! Much time can be lost, wasted, *et cetera*, if for some strange reason you choose *not* to heed this advice. Backtracking to this particular chapter from all others in the handbook may leave you with many frustrated students whom you will never recover while you try to regain your composure long enough to learn "The 1, 2, 3 of it." So, have this "under your belt" *before* beginning.

After reading through the step-by-step approach to storyboarding and after examining the sample format, you should be ready to tackle any one of the seven chapters with ease and success, no matter how limited a background you have with

35mm cameras, still photography, super 8mm movies, video tape recorders, or dry mount presses. The organization you derive from mastering storyboarding should give you enough confidence to learn right along with your students—and enjoy it at the same time.

OBJECTIVE

To learn the basic techniques involved in storyboarding any nonprint program.

STRATEGIES

One of the best ways, if perhaps not *the best way*, to learn this basic technique is to do it! Therefore, as you read through the procedure you are invited, encouraged, *urged* to try your hand, no matter how simple or ridiculous you may think it is (better to stay simple at first before attempting to tackle something too complex). Again, if you work through each step, this should give you the courage to try out the technique with students.

DEFINITION OF TERMS

Storyboarding: A process whereby the idea or subject to be developed is broken down into small segments which can be placed and rearranged until a desired, logical sequence is obtained; the individual segments usually contain some type of visual representation of what is to be seen, the proposed written script, if any, that accompanies the visual, and any particular instructions peculiar to that segment, such as the angle of the camera when taking the picture, music background and desired volume/tone, etc.

Scripting: The process of transferring the individual pieces of information from the storyboard cards onto a divided page where the visual is described and the narration is written out for each segment to be viewed; the two or three pages of script may be dittoed for distribution to the students for further reference.

Video: The picture to be visualized on the storyboard cards.

Audio: The written message or "script" that will accompany the visual on the storyboard cards.

MATERIALS AND COSTS

Storyboarding is an inexpensive activity in comparison to all of the nonprint productions covered in chapters two through seven. The only expense to be anticipated is the cost for pencils, 5"x8" note cards, and thumb tacks. You should attempt to buy cards no smaller than 5"x8" since you will need the space for a rough sketch of the subject to be visualized, the accompanying script, and any special instructions. If you are working with a class of some 30 students, you will probably want around three cards for each student so that the student can practice with the limitations of space on two of the cards and finally produce one that is suitable. Once *you* have tried your hand at this, you will become convinced that three cards per student is a minimum expenditure.

Item	Estimated Cost
5"x8" note cards	under $1.00
box of no. 2 pencils	under $1.00
thumb tacks	under $1.00
Total	under $3.00

PROCEDURE FOR PRODUCTION

The procedure section, although long, is a detailed, step-by-step account of the process involved to compile the information on a particular topic for nonprint production. The following steps are discussed: selecting the subject or idea, outlining the subject, storyboarding, and scripting.

A. Selecting the subject or idea

Perhaps the most difficult part of working through this activity and in producing the nonprint item in the handbook is deciding on *the* subject, *the* idea to develop. I have witnessed 50-50 splits in a classroom regarding the decision over which subject to storyboard that could never be resolved no matter how resourceful I was.

For your own protection and for the sake of class time, some pre-decisions need to be made by the person who is guiding the group activity—teacher *or* elected student:

a. have some suggested subjects, topics, ideas ready for consideration, and

b. keep these suggestions *simple*.

By having a number of ideas ready, you immediately give the impression that some forethought has gone into the activity. You may even be surprised that the group likes one of the ideas and is willing to give it a try. However, no matter how innovative or creative you think your ideas are, it is *always* good to allow the group to express what they want to do, what they need to learn, or what they are *interested* in learning. If you are able to gain their *interest* in the first project of storyboarding, you might be able to *guide* the students to select a subject for development which they need to master.

Another important point that merits a brief explanation is the need to keep *especially* the first storyboarding attempt as simple as possible. The whole idea behind using this technique is to be able when completed to see the entire presentation from start to finish, segment by segment, and to be able to identify any problems along the way *before* production begins. If you and/or your group makes the decision to tackle something too complex, you will become lost in a maze of a thousand-and-one storyboard cards that have very little meaning. Also, you will end up spending too much time on the technique, and interest in the final production might become seriously deflated. DECIDE ON A SIMPLE IDEA TO DEVELOP—at least for the first production.

Another consideration that must not be overlooked is the availability of materials for the chosen subject. If you are familiar with the resources of your media center, you have no problem; however, if you are not, have a media specialist present at your initial meetings to react to the variety of proposals. There is little reason for students to become excited over an idea if no information is available. Also, by having the media specialist available for comment, this will alert him/her to reserve the desired materials *before* the actual research on the topic begins.

B. Outlining the subject

Once a group decision has been made to proceed and develop a specific subject, additional decisions need to be made before storyboarding begins. Using the input from the entire group, outline the subject. Decide on a tentative title. List the objectives to be accomplished within the framework of the presentation. Making such a list should give you and your group a clearer idea of exactly what it is you wish to show visually and to write for the content. Decide on your audience. Are you putting together a presentation on a particular subject for the students' peer group, or for younger students, or possibly for parents to receive information? Such a decision needs to be made at the onset so that the content will be suitable for its audience. When you and your group have the following in front of you:

Title:

Objective(s):

Audience:

you are ready to begin breaking the subject or idea down into its parts in outline form—

I.

    A.

        1.
        2.

    B.
    C.

        1.
        2.

II.

    A.
    B.

        1.
        2.

            etc.

C. Storyboarding

Now that your outline is complete, you and your group of students are ready to begin storyboarding.

Steps

1.   Pass out three cards per student and have them divide each card into sections so that it looks like this:

Video	Audio	#
Special Instructions:		

5"

8"

By having each card identical, the entire unit when placed in proper sequence will be easier to visualize and read from beginning to end.

2.   Explain what is meant by the different divisions:

    a.   video—the picture

    b.   audio—the written message that goes with the picture

    c.   #—the number of the card so that it may be kept in sequence

    d.   special instructions—space allowed for any special effects desired, such as directions for taking the picture—close-up, head only, dissolve from one visual to another—or for recording with one or two voices or with a music background

Warn the students at this point *not* to begin filling in their cards since no decision has been made as to *who* will be responsible for *what* on the outline.

3.   Return to the outline. If the outline is too long or involved to be kept on the board, then a copy of it should be made available to each student. It is a good idea to have the student hand out these copies or record the outline so that once the areas of responsibility for a particular segment are divided up, he knows who comes before and after his segment.

4.   Verbally visualize the outline beginning with the first major point. By "verbally visualize" I mean ask and/or suggest pictures that would represent what is stated in the outline at present by phrases or sentences. Once a decision has been reached as to what should be visualized, ask for a volunteer to sketch the picture (no elaborate drawing in color or a photograph is necessary at this stage).

You are more than likely to have a variety of comments regarding the student's inability to draw anything. *Reaction*: "So what!" You are not asking for a Rembrandt; a stick figure is suitable. The storyboard is merely a sketch of the final product and is only to be used for guidance to check for the flow of ideas on your chosen subject. It is important that everyone become involved in this initial stage, since more than likely the individual student will want to try his hand with a production on his own once he has seen how easy the process is.

5.   Assign each student an "A," "B," "C," etc. under each roman numeral until all segments are assigned (if you have subdivided the sections into "1," "2," "3," then these should be assigned one per student). Encourage the students to use all three cards to develop their picture. Some may feel that an "A" or "B" needs to be subdivided into additional sub-units; perhaps this is the case and three pictures are needed to get the point across. However, also encourage them to write out the "audio" which describes their picture(s).

No hard and fast rule exists regarding the number of sentences or words in those sentences used to describe a picture. If a paragraph is needed to describe one picture, then more than likely this paragraph should be broken down into 2-3 sentences, each with an appropriate picture. If the medium to be used to display your pictures is slides, then a viewer may become bored by watching one slide while listening to an entire paragraph. On the other hand, if motion is being used—movies or television, then a paragraph may be needed in order to include the total motion demanded in that particular segment. This is where judgment plays in the picture *and* a willingness to experiment with the medium selected for the presentation.

Students may need more than three cards to work out their segment. If this is the case, they should be encouraged to ask for more until they are satisfied with their work.

6. Allow for plenty of in-class or out-of-class work time on this first stage. Creativity should *not* be rushed! Also, be prepared for the noise.

I have found that students become very excited over such projects and to "sit on" such enthusiasm would definitely be a mistake. Once they have completed one card, they will want to share the results of their labor with a neighbor or "check it out" with you. They should also be encouraged to check with the individual whose segment comes before and after their segment to make sure their picture-script (video-audio) agrees with others and is in sequence.

I am sure by now that you recognize the ease with which such a project as storyboarding could be accomplished by one person—you may want to storyboard an idea on your own *before* attempting the process with a group. However, the *purpose* of this entire handbook is to turn kids on to print using nonprint. For this reason, the ideas presented are always with a group in mind. Hopefully, if you have the courage to use these techniques, you will readily become convinced by the enthusiasm generated by the students that a group encounter is ultimately more worthwhile and rewarding.

7. Once the *first* draft of cards is completed (warning: there will be many more *drafts* before the final project is viewed), thumb tack the cards on a bulletin board using the outline as a guide for sequencing. When all of the cards are in place, you may want to record a sequence number in the upper right-hand corner next to #.

Some people prefer to use a complicated coding system, such as I.A., I.B.(1), etc., which is unnecessary. A simple 1, 2, 3 . . . is all that is really needed. You may want to have a lead card with the main divisions noted to help check on the balance of the presentation; i.e., I, II, III or section I, section II, section III. Again, the number of cards within each division or segment will depend on your judgment and that of the class. This balance, or lack of it, is easier to see once the cards are placed on the bulletin board. If you are doing a story, you may only need a brief beginning and ending—few cards—and more in the body of the story—a larger number of cards.

Practice—and a few mistakes—will help you judge how many cards to use with the selected topic.

8.   Leave the storyboard alone in its rough form for a few days. Ask the students to read and view what is displayed to check for transition from picture-to-picture and text-to-text.

If the finished product is to move from one point to another as smoothly as possible, this step is essential. By leaving the cards up for all to see, problems will become obvious.

9.   After the students have had time to react individually, bring the group together for a step-by-step look at each individual segment of the storyboard.

You may think that such time is wasted in both of these two steps; however, time spent at this stage will ultimately save hours later on once the actual shooting of shots and taping of script begins.

Anticipate the noise! You have allowed for thinking time; now each student will need to be heard. As you proceed from the first card to the last, be willing to move the cards from their original position to another. It is wise *not* to remove any numbers recorded in the upper right-hand corner until you have made the *final* decision to leave the storyboard *as is*. You may also find it necessary during this process to add to the cards already displayed or to delete some as the group decides on the development of the topic.

10.   The decision must be made! There is no way that you will ever be able to please the entire group regarding the order of the storyboard cards. If the majority of the students agree, then you should stop the rearranging, renumber for proper sequencing and begin writing the script.

D.   Scripting

For scripting to be consistent, it is best to have a committee volunteered or assigned. Kemp in *Planning and Producing Audiovisual Materials* calls the script "your detailed blueprint; the map which gives definite directions for your picture-taking, art work, or filming" (p. 42). This is exactly what it is—a map which must be completed *first* before any decision is made on the visuals to be used. Realizing that realistically not everyone can be involved in the process, it is a good idea to allow the "art" committee, the "photographic" committee, and the "taping" committee to begin making preliminary plans so they will be ready to move once the scripting is completed. Decisions such as the medium to be used, the props to be set up or even made, the equipment operation that must be understood and tested are all items which should be worked on before the script committee is ready to share their results.

One of the main reasons for having a script committee is to make the wording—the written manuscript—consistent in form. It is at this stage a lot of times that frustration sets in—and the right time for you to have some of the answers to their frustration.

Students are usually *extremely* enthusiastic when it comes to working on a production such as this; however, once they face their own limitations on developing a topic so that it is factually correct, they are bound to become frustrated if they *or* you are not aware that the information they need is probably in print—books, reference materials, the vertical file, or periodicals—just waiting for them to read. If the script committee has such a problem, this is the proper time for you to TURN KIDS ON TO PRINT USING NONPRINT. This is an excellent stage at which to bring the production wheels to a grinding halt for *all* committees and schedule a few research days in your media center. The script committee should be encouraged to share their problems and make the necessary assignments where information needs to be found before the script can be completed.

Students should be reminded that information they find on the topic should be placed in their own words and that they should copy down their source and the page number in case the script committee needs to check it later. Also, they should be asked to briefly describe any visual contained on the printed page in case the art committee needs help or a point of reference for drawing or photographing this section.

I am afraid that a number of teachers automatically react negatively to the word "research" when trying to apply it to students of varying ability levels. The bright or average student will, in all likelihood, not experience much difficulty at this state; however, the student who has a reading problem or for some reason is reluctant to become involved needs to be encouraged. For such students I have actually had to sit down and read to them and ask them in turn to repeat in their own words what I read. Once they have understood the passage, together we have written down the content for the script committee. The rewards of such patience are numerous. Not only do such students feel that they are still very much a part of the group activity and are contributing with a report on their findings, but they are the ones who, as a result of such a positive experience, are not nearly as reluctant to ask for help or who willingly express a desire to have another, and yet another, passage explained to them when trying to discover information on their own.

When the research is completed and turned in to the script committee, they are ready to complete the final product and turn it over in duplicate to the other committees. It is at this stage that all of the remaining chapters in the handbook begin, since there is a certain degree of variability depending on the medium to be used.

SAMPLE FORMAT FOR STORYBOARDING

A.   Selecting the subject or idea

1.   How to make an apple cobbler — too complex; break this down into parts and select one

2.   Techniques for peeling an apple — simple; can be broken down into small segments; a good beginning activity to learn storyboarding

B.   Outlining the subject

Title: Techniques for peeling an apple — only a working title which may change a number of times before the final production

Objectives:
To show the variety of ways an apple can be peeled

To help others learn how to be safe when using sharp objects

To peel an apple so that it can be eaten or used for cooking

List all of the objectives students suggest. These will change and be refined once a direction is clarified by the group.

Audience: Elementary students: 2nd and 3rd grades — This will help the group determine the items to be used for the actual presentation.

Outline

I.   Items needed—preparation— first step
A.   Apple
B.   Tools
1. towels
2. apron
3. knives
4. peelers
4. saws

The first outline is a brainstorming experience in which everything is listed as fast as students think of it. Rearrangement can take place afterwards.

II.   The techniques
    A.   Peeling
       1. holding the apple
       2. which end do you begin with?
       3. care in handling the tools
    B.   Cutting the apple
       1. removing the core
       2. reasons for cutting
          a. eating
          b. cooking

III. The cleanup
    A.   Disposing of the peeling and core
    B.   Cleaning the counter and utensils

IV.   Eating the results

When the outline is complete, students need to re-examine once again the audience, the objectives to be accomplished, and zero in on a title that adequately represents the topic. The final outline which you and your group produce should be refined enough so that it will not have to be reworked again once the storyboarding begins. For this reason, I have found that when developing a topic such as this, and there are a variety of very simple ones to be developed, it is always best to *do* it with the class before making any revisions on the outline. Actually have one of the students visualize and verbalize the process in front of the class to check the outline on the board.

A refined outline might look something like this:

Title: The Apple—peel it . . . eat it . . . but be safe in the process!

Objective: To show how to peel an apple and be safe at the same time.

Audience: 2nd and 3rd grade students

Outline

I.   Preparation
    A.   Gathering the items
       1. towels
       2. apron
       3. knife
       4. dish
       5. apple

(Outline is continued on page 28)

B. Cleaning the apple
   1. wash
   2. dry

II. Process
   A. Peeling the apple
   B. Quartering the apple
   C. Cutting out the core

III. Final stage
   A. Eating
   B. Cleaning up
      1. throwing peeling and core away
      2. washing utensils

C. Storyboarding

One of the cards completed by a student might look like this:

Video	Audio	#11
	Dry	

Special Instructions: Close-up

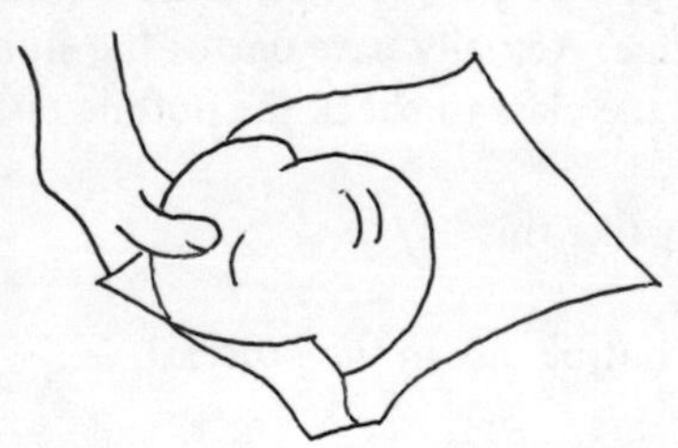

When displayed on the bulletin board, it is easier to see the entire development of the topic from beginning to end:

D.   Scripting

Visual	Narration

1.   Title: The Apple
            . . . peel it
            . . . eat it
         . . . but be safe in the process!
	The Apple . . . peel it . . . eat it . . . but be safe in the process!

2. PREPARATION	Certain steps need to be considered before eating an apple. This is known as preparation.

(Continued on page 30)

Visual	Narration
3. Girl looking in cabinet for items.	If you decide to peel an apple, there are a number of items you will need before you begin.
4. Close-up of hands holding paper towels.	You will need paper towels to dry the apple off.
5. Girl putting on apron.	To protect your clothes, you might want to put an apron on.
6. Close-up of hands holding a kitchen knife.	You need to be very careful when handling the knife you will use to peel the apple.
7. Close-up of hands with bowl.	You should also have a bowl of some type to catch the peelings and core of the apple once you begin.
8. Apple on counter.	Last but not least, you need the apple.
9. Girl standing at sink with water running.	Before peeling the apple, it is a good to clean it thoroughly.
10. Close-up of water running over the apple.	Wash the apple with water to remove any dirt or insect spray.
11. Close-up of using towel to dry the apple.	Take the towels you have placed beside the sink and completely dry the apple.
12. PROCESS	Now you are ready for the process of peeling the apple.
13. Close-up of hands holding apple and knife.	Hold the apple firmly and peel the apple with the knife starting at the stem end and moving slowly around the apple. Take your time and be careful to cut the apple and not your finger.

(Continued on page 31)

Visual	Narration
14. Close-up of apple split in half and hands holding one section with knife half way down on section.	Once the apple has been peeled, cut the apple in two equal sections and then again into quarters. This will make it easier to remove the core where the seeds are.
15. Close-up of hands holding one section while removing core.	Take each quarter and cut out the core or center of the apple.
16. FINAL STAGE	Now you are ready for the final stage of the process.
17. Girl eating a section of the apple.	You can now enjoy eating the apple you have taken such care to peel.
18. Long shot of girl carrying bowl and utensils to the trash.	You should not forget that cleaning up is part of the process too.
19. Girl emptying peelings and core into trash can.	Throw the peeling and core into a trash can.
20. Girl standing at sink washing the bowl and the knife.	The final step is washing the dish and the knife used. Again, be careful not to cut your fingers when washing the knife.

Notice that the description of the visuals listed on the script are taken from the sketches on the storyboard (video) which have been developed from the ideas listed on the outline. The actual narration (audio) which will accompany the visuals is also an expansion of the outline. Care should always be taken to keep the grade level(s) and the specific objective(s) in mind when writing the narration for the presentation. Such a production could ultimately become a filmstrip with an audio tape, a slide/tape, an 8mm movie, or a brief television show. The format and equipment to be used will depend to a great extent on your willingness to experiment with various media; your students will want to explore all of the above!

SUGGESTIONS FOR FOLLOW-UP ACTIVITIES

The following topics, some of which demand a certain amount of research by the student before they can be completed, are only suggestions for an initial investigation into storyboarding. Again, remember, the best experience is the one which is simple.

Topics

1. Frying an egg
2. Sharpening a pencil
3. Washing dishes
4. Cutting grass
5. Making a terrarium
6. Proper grooming
7. From seedling to tree
8. Changing seasons
9. Writing a paper
10. Making a puppet
11. Changing a tire
12. Metric measures
13. Parts of a book
14. Differences: Circle, Square, and Triangle
15. Planting a garden
16. How to take a picture
17. From egg to chicken
18. Making ice cream
19. Development of a frog
20. Putting on makeup

Note that the topics vary in difficulty; some are suitable for younger students and others for older—you and your students' interests will help to determine the best topic to storyboard.

ANNOTATED BIBLIOGRAPHY

Brown, James W., and Richard B. Lewis, Eds. *AV Instructional Technology Manual for Independent Study.* 5th ed. New York: McGraw-Hill, 1977, pp. 59-60.
Storyboarding is briefly discussed in relation to "developing one-screen slide presentations." Pictures are included.

Brown, James W., Richard B. Lewis, and Fred F. Harcleroad. *AV Instruction— Technology, Media, and Methods.* 5th ed. New York: McGraw-Hill, 1977, pp. 158-60.
Storyboarding is defined and illustrated visually. Information on "script shorthand" is also given.

Kemp, Jerrold E. *Planning and Producing Audiovisual Materials.* 3rd ed. New York: Thomas Y. Crowell, 1975, pp. 51-58.
Detailed coverage is given to storyboarding as a technique to be used in all aspects of producing audiovisual programs. An entire chapter titled "Mapping the Way" is devoted to the subject. Pictures are included.

Wittich, Walter A., and Charles F. Schuller. *Instructional Technology: Its Nature and Use.* 5th ed. New York: Harper and Row, 1973, pp. 493-94.
A brief overview of storyboarding is given with particular emphasis on "pupil planning for film-making." Illustrations of the technique are included.

SUPPLIERS OF EQUIPMENT AND SOFTWARE

In the case of storyboarding, the items needed—pencils, 5"x8" cards, and thumb tacks—can be purchased from almost any book or discount store. In many instances, I am sure that the school stocks most of the items.

A new product from Visual Horizons, 208 Westfall Road, Rochester, New York 14620, is the "Audio Image Planner." Their storyboard arrangement is essentially the same as discussed in this chapter, yet they have a ring binder which holds the 5½"x8½" pages together and each page has an original and two carbonless pages which may be removed and displayed. The planner kit which contains 1 binder, 100 carbonless, and 100 bond pages costs $7.25.

Courtesy of Visual Horizons

CHAPTER 2

FILMSTRIP PRESENTATIONS

Frank Borman Elementary
Denton, Texas

CHAPTER 2

FILMSTRIP PRESENTATIONS

INTRODUCTION

Making a filmstrip for pleasure and/or for a particular reason, such as for placement in the school media center or for viewing by parents at a parent-teachers meeting, can be and *should* be tackled by any age group. You should remember that the underlying reason for producing all of these nonprint items is to entice students to make more use of the printed page. The key to success is planning the entire sequence of events—from deciding on the topic to the actual presentation. If you organize FIRST you still might experience some rough going along the way, but the likelihood of having a smoother transition from one stage to another is greatly increased.

I have seen some of the best filmstrips come out of a kindergarten class, simply because the teacher knew the level of the students and worked *within* it. On the other hand, I have seen second grade teachers almost in tears and students highly frustrated because the expectation level was set too high. For example, if after storyboarding your topic, you find that the students simply cannot draw the pictures they wish to represent the narration, then allow them to use magazine pictures which they have cut up and arranged on the page or let them use tracing paper to trace the pictures from a book. A gifted art teacher might shudder at this suggestion, but the purpose of all of these productions is to "turn kids on"—not off! By all means, enjoy making filmstrips, and the pleasure you and your students receive from the experience will be evident in the final product.

OBJECTIVES

To learn the process involved and the equipment to be used in making a filmstrip.

To learn how to record the narration so that it is synchronized with each filmstrip frame.

STRATEGIES

My initial introduction in making filmstrips with students came about as a result of a teacher's frustration in working with a low ability group. As mentioned in my AVI article (see Turning Kids On to Print, page 13), she had tried every method possible to get her students to read. I suggested making a filmstrip which would require them to read from a number of printed sources found in the media center.

To motivate these students, check out a commercially produced filmstrip from the media center that has an accompanying cassette tape and show this to the class *without* explaining why. Once you have finished, ask them: "I wonder how difficult it would be to make a filmstrip with a cassette tape of our own, using a subject you want to develop?" Expect an explosion of enthusiastic yells from a captive audience. While you have them and before you select your idea for storyboarding, review the filmstrip/tape and have them comment on how the presentation was put together, the pictures, the narration and any background music, *et cetera*. If they understand from the beginning that the task is not easy and cannot be accomplished overnight, then they should be able to settle down to the steps to achieve the finished product.

Once you have the finished filmstrip/tape on file in your permanent collection, it can be used over and over again to motivate other students. More than likely you will not even have to advertise it—you will be approached by students who know by word-of-mouth that you have accomplished this feat and as a result they cannot wait until they have the opportunity to produce their own.

DEFINITION OF TERMS

Filmstrip: A continuous roll of developed film with pictures on the film

correctly spaced so that when placed in a filmstrip projector or viewer they may be seen one at a time; since the film is 35mm, sprockets will be down both sides so that the finished product may be used in a projector or viewer.

35mm SLR camera: A single(S) lens(L) reflex(R) camera which takes 35mm film and allows the viewer (you), when looking through the camera, to see exactly what will be recorded on the film.

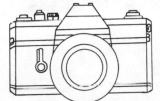

Close-up rings: Extender rings which increase the focus power of your camera so that it (the lens) will focus closer to the picture; this will allow you to focus on the smallest of pictures; +1, +2, or +4 extender rings added to your lens will enable you to copy a picture down to 4"x6".

Cassette tape recorder: A tape recorder which will accept individual cassettes varying in recording time from 30-90 minutes; some units have built-in microphones; others have microphones that can be held or propped on a stand.

Copy stand: Equipment which is designed to hold the camera parallel and above the pictures; when you use a copy stand and camera, you will want to have a cable release so as not to shake the camera when taking the pictures.

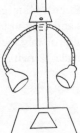

Cable release: An attachment which screws into the shutter release mechanism and keeps you from jarring the camera when taking the picture.

Tripod: A three-pronged stand which allows you to screw the camera on top; a cable release should also be used with this once the pictures are framed and in focus.

MATERIALS AND COSTS

The cost of materials will vary somewhat depending on your locale; however, by shopping wisely and comparing prices from at least three distributors for each item, you should be able to save dollars.

Equipment

A.   Camera

Almost any 35mm SLR camera is suitable for copy work. I have a preference for a certain brand name—Canon; yet I have just recently purchased a Minolta for class use. Both cameras have a standard f/1.7 or 1.8 50 mm lens and built-in light meter. Both sell for under two hundred dollars (a price that will probably increase in the next few years). I have never invested in close-up rings made particularly for copy work.

B.   Close-up rings

Also called extender rings or magnifying lenses, close-up rings will fluctuate in price depending upon the 35mm camera you purchase. For most cameras you can purchase an adapter which will allow you to use a variety of different makes of close-up rings. Each ring (+1, +2, or +4) which moves the focus of the larger lens closer to the picture will cost around $5.00 each. Total cost for all four items is approximately $20.00.

C.   Copy stand

A copy stand that will serve your needs should not exceed one hundred dollars. If you do comparative shopping *with your camera* in hand to check for placement of the camera on the stand, you will probably be able to find a durable stand for around $50.

D.   Tripod

Again, using comparative pricing and proper investigation, a tripod should not cost any more than $30. The same tripod can be used with the super 8mm camera and video television camera, so you are buying one item to serve three needs.

E.   Cable release

A cable release should run no more than $5.00 and may be purchased from almost any dealer selling photographic equipment.

F.   Cassette tape recorder

Beware. There are such a wide variety of recorders on the market, some with an all-too-short life span. Buying either Sony, Panasonic, or Wollensak should insure that you have quality and durability. You are going to pay more for any of these recorders, but in the long run you will not regret your purchase since it can be used for a variety of other productions. A reasonable price would be around $75-$100.

G.   Filmstrip projector and/or viewer

Bell and Howell, Singer, and Graflex are only three of the reputable leaders in the filmstrip projector field. A projector produced by one of these companies should not exceed $150. A variety of combinations can be purchased in the projector/viewer line. If you decide to make such a purchase, I always advise buying the *complete* package so that you have not only a projector/viewer but also a recorder/player all in one. The cost is not prohibitive if you consider that you have 1) a projector, 2) a viewer, 3) a recorder, and 4) a player. Current prices for this item range from $350-$400.

Software

A. Cassette tapes

Most discount or drug stores carry cassette tapes. You pay not only for the recording time but also for the quality of the product. A 60-minute tape (each side is 30 minutes) should cost around $1.50 or less.

B. Film

35mm film either 20 exposures or 36 exposures may be purchased from discount stores or photographic dealers. Prices will vary very little among slide films.

C. Processing

Developing the slide film depending on the number of exposures (20-36) will range in price from $2.50-$4.00. The quality of the picture depends to a great extent on the processor, so choose one that you know is reliable for this quality.

SUMMARY LIST OF ESTIMATED COSTS

Equipment

Item	Estimated Cost
camera	$200
close-up rings	20
copy stand	50
tripod	30
cable release	5
cassette tape recorder	75
filmstrip projector	150
projector/viewer/recorder	350

A projector/viewer/recorder is not necessary if you have a cassette tape recorder and a filmstrip projector.

Software

cassette tapes	$1.50 each
film (20 exposures-36 exposures)	2.50-4.00 each
processing	2.00-3.50 each

Software prices will vary greatly depending on your shopping ability and sometimes the area in which you live.

PROCEDURE FOR PRODUCTION

You are ready to begin working on the filmstrip if and *only if* you have completed the storyboard and scripting on a particular topic. Once you and the students are pleased with the flow of pictures and ideas roughly sketched on the storyboard cards and with the filming directions and narration of the script, you should introduce the following procedures for production of the filmstrip: art work, format, content, and size of the pictures; choice of films; loading the film; placement of pictures; using the copy stand or tripod; photographing the pictures; taping the narration; and the showing.

1. Art work. The basic decision to be reached before any work begins is who will be responsible for the actual pictures to be photographed. Does the class wish to contribute individually or do they want an art committee responsible for all the pictures? There are advantages and disadvantages to either of the two choices. If the entire group contributes, students feel a real sense of accomplishment when they view their pictures on the screen *or* they may feel a sense of embarrassment. If an art committee produces all of the pictures, the final production will probably be more consistent in form and look like what it was meant to look like, yet this may cut down on the enthusiasm of the group. You need to know the desire and *ability* of your particular group of students.

2. Format of the pictures. The entire class should also be involved in making the decision on the format of the pictures. You have at least two choices to make:
    a.   will the pictures be *copied* from existing photographs, traced, from magazines, or will they be originals; and
    b.   what medium will be used: crayon, pencil, felt-tip pens, watercolors, tempra, or woodcuts?

A factor which helps to determine the answer to both of these questions is the age group with which you are working. A kindergarten group might become highly frustrated if they decided to make original tempra paintings, or a senior high group might be insulted if required to cut and paste pictures from a magazine.

3. Content of the pictures. Students need to be cautioned regarding the content of the pictures to be projected. If too much is jammed into one picture, there is no way the viewer can possibly take in the total display. Also, the colors used in the pictures should offer contrast and not be so dark that a person standing in the foreground of a picture could not be distinguished from the background. The video portion of your storyboard should be clear enough to help direct the student in selection of proper content.

4.   Size of the pictures. Students need adequate space on which to produce their visuals. As long as they keep their drawing horizontal on a
3:4 ratio no problem will be encountered. Standard typing or construction
paper may be used as long as the student is told to keep the drawing
centered.

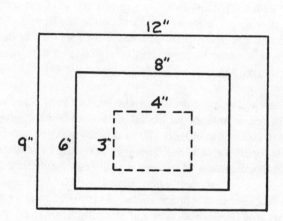

5.   Helpful hints
    a.   If you are working with a young group of students, you will
probably want to encourage them to work from magazine or
coloring book pictures. They may want to add color to their pictures with crayon, watercolor, or tempra. More advanced students
might try tracing pictures from other sources. Tracing paper may
be bought or the inside sheet of a ditto thermal stencil may be
used—at no expense to you. Once the student has traced the
picture and has the desired colors marked on the drawing, it can
easily be transferred to regular typing or construction paper with
carbon paper or the ink sheet of a ditto master—again, at no
additional expense.
    b.   As the drawings are completed, make sure you number them
on the back according to the script you will be using for the
narration and taping. Check off each drawing on a master script
as you record the number; this will help you and the class see
how the illustrations are proceeding and who has not finished the
assignment.

6.   Choice of film. The film you buy should be slide film: kodachrome or
ektachrome. Brands of slide film other than Kodak are also suitable. If you
are using a copy stand or tripod with artificial light, a high speed tungsten
film is best, such as ektachrome 160 (tungsten). If you are shooting inside
without artificial light using only the existing light from windows, you will
also want a higher speed film, such as ASA 200 high speed ektachrome

daylight film. If you go outside and use natural light, then you can use one of the kodachrome films with a lower ASA of 25 or 64.

If you desire additional information on the different types of film, refer to the *Amateur's Photographer's Handbook*, 8th edition (T. Y. Crowell, 1973. $9.95) by Aaron Sussman.

7.   Loading the film in your camera. Once you have purchased the 35mm camera, you must know either from being told by your dealer or from reading the enclosed instructions how to load the film. This is not an instamatic camera which receives only one type of plastic cartridge, so you will need to practice this before the actual shooting begins.

Once you have loaded the film, be sure to check the box it came in for the ASA number, such as ASA 25, 64, 160, 200, and so on. Set the ASA dial of your camera to match the ASA on the film box (see the picture below; most cameras are similar enough so that you can easily locate and adjust this dial).

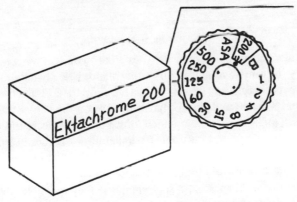

8.   Placement of pictures for photographing. In case you have not realized by now, every time you snap the camera you will actually be producing two frames for your filmstrip. Therefore, if you have a 20-exposure roll of film, you will have a capacity for a 40-frame filmstrip; a 36-exposure roll could yield a 72-frame filmstrip.

Standard filmstrip projectors that you use every day are made to project only a certain area of the film. By photographing two pictures each time, you will produce a filmstrip that is on exactly the same format as the projector you will be using. *Do not panic*; it is really quite easy to make a filmstrip if you carefully follow the instructions below.

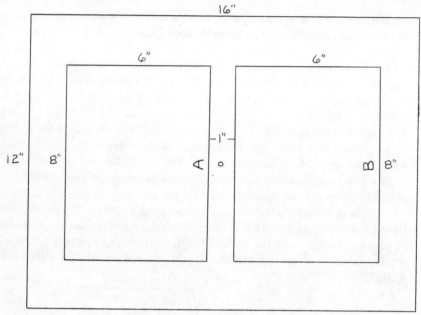

Camera Mounted on Tripod: Layout Arrangement

If your students have made their pictures 3"x4" you will want to use the format above with your camera mounted on a copy stand. Use a black or gray piece of construction paper measuring at least 12"x16". Find the exact center by measuring in 6 inches and 8 inches and glue a small red circle on the center point. Draw two parallel lines 8 inches in length in pencil 1-inch apart; measure out 6 inches more in both directions and draw two more parallel lines 8 inches in length. Label the first rectangle A and the second B. The *bottom* of all odd number pictures will be placed on A, and the *bottom* of all even numbered pictures will be placed on B. If your pictures are larger than 3"x4", for example if they are 6"x8", 9"x12", or 12"x16", use the same set up as mentioned above for 1-inch between pictures. You will also need a larger piece of construction paper for the background and your camera mounted on a tripod.

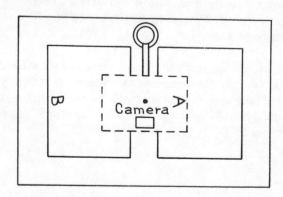

Whether to use a copy stand or tripod with the 35mm SLR camera will depend on the size of your pictures. If your students have drawn their pictures 3"x4", you will want to use the copy stand; however, anything larger than 3"x4" you will have to use a tripod. If your pictures are smaller than 3"x4", you will need to invest in the close-up rings defined at the beginning of this chapter. Warning: I would *not* advise having students work within a picture area any smaller than 6"x8" simply because anything smaller than this becomes tedious and difficult.

9. Photographing the pictures.
   a. Camera on copy stand. Mount the 35mm camera on the copy stand, making sure the light meter in the camera is working by turning on the two lights attached to the copy stand and moving your hand back and forth in front of the lens. This action should make the meter needle move.

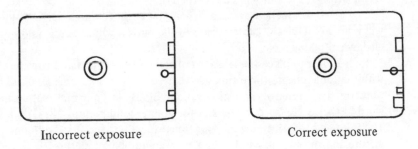

Incorrect exposure   Correct exposure

By working with your camera, you should know when the meter indicates that you have adjusted your lens to allow for enough light to fall onto the film.

Place the black or gray construction paper background you made in step No. 8 on the base of the copy stand. When you look through the lens of your camera, the circle should be in the center, A on your right and B on your left.

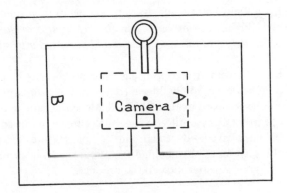

Allow for about the same margin around the outside of both pictures as the 1-inch space that separates them in the middle. You will have to move the arm of the copy stand up or down until you have this margin in alignment. Once you have done this, you should tape the edges of the construction paper down so that it will not move once you begin.

For best results place the first two pictures under the camera and flat on the base of the copystand. Focus the pictures and adjust the meter. Then place a piece of gray paper on top of the original pictures. Readjust the meter reading for the gray; this will allow for all of the tones between white and black to be taken into account and is actually a more accurate and true reading of the pictures you will be taking.

You will also want to position the lights on either side of the camera so that there is no glare or hot spot shining directly onto the pictures. Simply keep working with this until you are satisfied. Usually positioning the lights at 45° angles to the pictures is satisfactory. Remember that what you are seeing through the lens will be recorded on the film, so *take your time.*

To avoid camera movement when you begin filming your shots, you will want to attach the cable release to the button which you would normally click when taking a picture.

It is best to place the lens cover back on the camera and trip the shutter with the cable release three times so that you have a six frame lead to your filmstrip. Then remove the lens cover and insert for your first picture the word "FOCUS" in large letters and for your second picture "BEGIN TAPE." The third and fourth frame of your filmstrip will be the first odd-numbered picture and the second will be the first even-numbered picture.

Proceed slowly when filming. Check the order of the pictures and the placement each time *before* snapping the cable release. If you make a mistake—START OVER. This is the major reason for taking your time, since you cannot rearrange the sequence as you would if you were taking slides. When you have finished filming, re-roll the film in the camera back into its container.

Keep the student-made drawings on file until you have received the processed film back from the dealer. *Be sure to inform the processor that this is a filmstrip and must not be cut and mounted into slides.*

b.   Camera on a tripod. The same process can be used with the tripod; however, you will have to mount your construction background on a bulletin board or flannel board. Move the camera on the tripod closer or farther away until you have the center in focus and left-right margins in line. I have used straight pins to hold pictures in place, but I have also seen tape rolled behind the pictures which is time consuming but also gives a neater look to the product.

10. Taping the narration. Time can be saved while the filmstrip is being developed by practicing the narration for taping. It is best to line the students up with shoes removed and with a copy of what each is to say in sequence. If the class decides to use only two or three readers, then you can place them around the microphone in a semicircle for taping.

So that the individual operating the filmstrip projector will know when to turn each frame, it is best to record a "ping" at the end of the frame. The first "ping" should come at the beginning of the tape when the filmstrip is in FOCUS and thereafter until the viewing is completed. A glass or triangle may be used to create the "ping" sound. If you have more sophisticated equipment, you may want to pulse the tape with an inaudible signal once the recording is completed.

Stress the importance of not stopping once the tape has been started; if you do, you will hear a click in the tape each time you stop or start it. If you tape each practice run, you are bound to get one "take" that is good. This can easily be copied onto another cassette tape so that it will be at the beginning of the cassette.

11. The showing. If at all possible, share the filmstrip/tape FIRST with the class that produced it. You can tell by holding it up to a light if the filmstrip is good—are the pictures in proper sequence and right side up? Expect quite a bit of noise when they see and hear the presentation. Much effort has gone into the work and the students will want to enjoy their masterpiece.

12. Copying the filmstrip and tape. To protect the original filmstrip and tape you might want to make a copy of both for your permanent collection and/or the media center. Making a copy of the tape is the easiest part. Simply use another cassette tape recorder with a microphone *or* use a special direct hookup known as a patch cord. From the original tape use "auxiliary out" to "auxiliary in" on the other tape recorder. You will have essentially the same quality tape as the original.

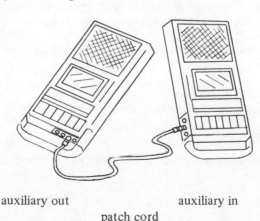

auxiliary out   auxiliary in
patch cord

Making a copy of the original filmstrip is not as easy. For best results, you should write to the following addresses and request a price check on the copying of an original filmstrip. The price will range from $20.00 for *one* copy to $4.50 for multiple copies *after* the first copy:

Stokes Slide Services
7000 Cameron Road
Austin, Texas 78752

Lowell T. Nerge
11941 Jefferson St. N.E.
Minneapolis, Minn. 55434

You might also want to ask your photographic dealer how much they would charge for the process. Also, if you know in advance that you want extra copies, it is much cheaper in the long run to make them at the same time you are shooting the original filmstrip simply by repeating the process for each copy.

SAMPLE FORMAT AND
EVALUATION FOR MAKING A FILMSTRIP

The following, "A School of Dolls" and "Adventures in the Forest", represent a report of an individual project completed by an elementary librarian for a graduate course in library science. Note the completeness of her report and the step-by-step procedure she used in working with the students in order to produce the final product.

DIARY:

MAKING A FILMSTRIP

Steps

1. Discuss with group of boys and girls about working on an original story project with magazine pictures as illustrations. The teachers and I decided to work with a middle ability group of third graders.

2. Analyze structure of several easy books with children so that the students will have a guide.

3. Rough in a storyboard—story line and the general idea of a dialog in order to know what kind of pictures to look for as illustrations.

4. Select pictures.

5. Produce illustrations: cut, paste pictures and decide on sequence using storyboard.

6. With pictures, write down dialog in detail.

7. Photograph illustrations.

8. Practice reading of script before making tape.

9. Make final tape.

	Time	
Activity	Boys	Girls
We discussed several books such as *Corduroy* by Don Freeman, *Whistle for Willie* by Ezra Jack Keats, and *Milton the Early Riser* by Robert Kraus. We noted the authors followed a three step pattern. They presented a problem or situation which was then developed and finally resolved.	20 min.	20 min.
The boys and girls wanted to separate and work on different stories. The roughing out of a story line went smoothly, each	20 min.	20 min.
group taking about twenty minutes or so. The drafting of dialogs took about twenty to forty minutes each.	30-50 min.	30-50 min.
It was when we came to the selection of pictures that we ran into trouble. It was difficult to find the pictures needed for their "plots." The children looked in stacks of magazines from beauty parlors and homes. The search took longer than we had anticipated.	3 hours	3 hours
The cutting, pasting, and printing presented no problems. As the children worked on the pictures, they also refined the dialogs here and there.	2 hours	3 hours
The media specialist helped with photographing the pictures.	1½ hours	1½ hours
The practice reading and taping were made with a few more changes.	1 hour	1 hour
The final taping took longer than I had thought. By this time the children were quite particular about how they sounded.	½ hour	1 hour
	9½ hours	12 hours

EVALUATION

Strengths

The Children:

1.   were made more aware of the structure of stories

2.   had experience in group work and the writing of a simple dialog

3.   learned something of proportion and relationship of pictures

4.   practiced speaking distinctly

5.   felt a sense of accomplishment and had a good time.

The Librarian:

6.   learned about the use of a camera and the set up for taking pictures.

Weaknesses

1.   The search for pictures was very time consuming. Perhaps we should have had more flexible story lines, but the children did not want to change their original plans too much.

2.   Ignorance of the librarian about camera techniques. I was most fortunate to have the help of the media specialist.

SCRIPT:

SCHOOL FOR DOLLS

Readers: Lisa, Rhonda, Pam, and Amy

Lisa: Hey, let's play school with our dolls.

Rhonda: Uh-oh, I think we've lost them.

Pam: I wonder where they are.

PING

Amy: I don't see them. Are they under the sofa?

PING

Lisa: No. Maybe they're in the dining room.

Rhonda: We'd better not go in there. Mother has everything fixed up pretty for her party tonight.

PING

Pam: Let's look in the kitchen.

Amy: Mother said, "Don't dare put a foot on that wet floor."

PING

Lisa: Here's the sun room. They might be in here.

Rhonda: No such luck.

PING

Pam: I'm going in the bedroom.

PING

Amy: I'll check the guest bedroom.

Lisa: Did you find our dolls?

Pam and Amy: No.

PING

Rhonda: I've already been in the play room. They're not there.

PING

Pam: Do you suppose they could be in the garden?

PING

Amy: I have a good idea. Maybe they are in the attic.

Lisa: I think your grandmother is cleaning up there.

PING

Rhonda: There they are!

PING

Pam: Here are the new books your mother bought.

PING

Amy: There are our toys, games and alphabets for our dolls.

PING

Lisa: I really love our doll furniture.

PING

Rhonda: We have everything for our doll's school. Let's play.

Everyone: O.K.

PING

THE END

ADVENTURE IN THE FOREST

Readers: James, Tommy, and Chris

James: We've been walking in the forest for a long time it seems to me.

Tommy: Do you suppose we've been walking in circles?

Chris: I'm getting tired. I hope we can find a place to camp soon.

PING

James: Oh, a red dog.

Tommy: That's not a dog. That's a fox.

Chris: I surely hope he doesn't see that fawn.

PING

James: There's a bear and her cubs. We better get out of here before that mother starts chasing us.

PING

Tommy: Oh, no! Look at that snake. I don't like snakes any better than momma bears.

PING

Chris: Wow! Did you see those pretty rocks?

PING

James: That's the biggest turkey I ever saw. I'd like to cook and eat him.

PING

Tommy: What a pretty bird! I think it's a grosbeak.

PING

Chris: Thank goodness, we're out of the woods.

PING

(Continued on page 56)

James: Let's go beyond that boy flying his kite.

PING

Tommy: We'll be able to swim and go boating.

PING

Chris: We'd better hurry and set up our tent and unroll our sleeping bags.

PING

James: Good night.

Tommy: Good night.

Chris: Good night.

PING

THE END

—Isabelle Scruggs

ANNOTATED BIBLIOGRAPHY

Brown, James W., and Richard B. Lewis, Eds. *AV Instructional Technology Manual for Independent Study.* 5th ed. New York: McGraw-Hill, 1977, pp. 53-56.
Authors discuss how to make "films without cameras" and "copying with a still camera." Well-illustrated showing drawing on film and students using copy stand equipment.

Brown, James W., Richard B. Lewis, and Fred F. Harcleroad. *AV Instruction: Technology, Media, and Methods.* 5th ed. New York: McGraw-Hill, 1977, pp. 194-95.
Authors include a section on "uses of filmstrips by individuals" and also a section on "producing handmade filmstrips." Illustrations are given which display the process.

Brown, Richard. "Exciting? Dramatic? Filmstrips?" *Film Library Quarterly* (Spring 1970):19-22.
Author investigates the variety of approaches to make filmstrips more enjoyable and meaningful for the viewers. "Narration without lip-sync" is explained. Methods to "avoid a static quality" are also explored.

Cloke, William. "Filmstrips—How to Make Your Own." *California School Libraries* (Winter 1976):15-18.
In very straight, simple language, the author step-by-step explains "what you need to get started," "film," "lenses," "title and theme," "photocopy stand," "titles and inserts," "arrangement of slides," and "sound and narration." Illustrations of limited value.

Hatch, Lawrence A. "Making and Testing a Filmstrip." *California School Libraries* (Spring 1973):6-9.
The author briefly discusses the process involved in making a filmstrip and then testing its suitability for the intended audience. An unusual view of the considerations that directly influence filmstrip production is given. Illustrations show planning and storyboarding involved.

Kemp, Jerrold E. *Planning and Producing Audiovisual Materials.* 3rd ed. New York: Thomas Y. Crowell, 1975, pp. 184-91.
The author devotes an entire chapter to filmstrips: "types," "special considerations when planning," "difficulties to overcome," "making a filmstrip by direct filming," " . . . from slides," " . . . by copying illustrations and photographs," and "correlating with narration." Numerous helpful illustrations are given.

McBride, Otis. "Local Production with 35mm Photography." *School Libraries* (Winter 1971):25-27.
Basic information regarding the camera and film is given. Details are explained, such as meanings of "rangefinder," "exposure meter," "viewfinder," "focus," "shutter," and "stops." Sequencing pictures for photographing is diagrammed. Illustrated.

Turner, Philip M. *Handbook for In-school Media Personnel.* Green Bay, WI: PLT Publications, 1975, pp. 44-49.
Helpful hints and proper copying techniques are explained. Illustrations are simple and would be useful for the individual that needs additional basic knowledge before attempting the technique.

Vitz, Carol. "Recipe for a Filmstrip." *California School Libraries* (Spring 1976): 19-26.
The author gives a detailed list of the "basic ingredients" and the process of putting a finished filmstrip together. Some of the problems of having a commercial sponsor for the filmstrip are also presented. Illustrations not appropriate to the text.

Wittich, Walter A., and Charles F. Schuller. *Instructional Technology: Its Nature and Use.* 5th ed. New York: Harper and Row, 1973, p. 405.
Brief coverage is given to the advantages of making a filmstrip by teachers and students for class use.

SUGGESTIONS FOR FOLLOW-UP ACTIVITIES

1. Show the filmstrip/tape to another class. Have the students answer questions relating to the storyboarding and production procedures.

2. Send notices home by the students that a special showing will be held for all parents.

3. Let the students display the pictures with the accompanying narration for each on a bulletin board used in the filmstrip.

4. Now that you have been successful with using a camera to photograph your pictures for a finished filmstrip, you should try another method perhaps as satisfying—drawing directly on 35mm film using pencils, transparency marking pens, or water-soluble oil colors.

If the media specialist has damaged filmstrips in the media center which can no longer be used because the lead has torn sprockets or the filmstrip has been ripped in half, trim away the damaged ends and bleach the film. Place the film in a mixture of one cup of bleach and a sink of warm water until the strip is clear. Wash the film completely and allow to dry. Draw the following on a piece of heavy cardboard and cut along the dotted lines with a single-edged razor blade:

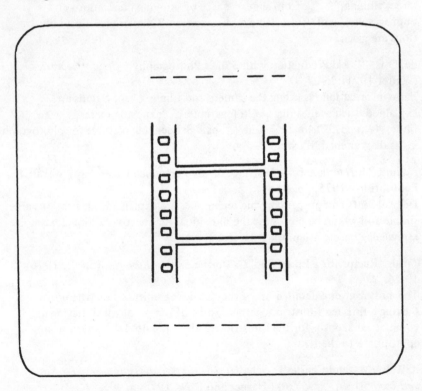

Trace this and transfer on cardboard with carbon paper.

Allow for a 5-frame lead to the filmstrip. You may want to have students draw
their presentation directly onto the film without marking the individual blocks. If
this is the case, you need to remind them that they cannot go beyond the area
since this is all that will be projected. I prefer to draw the blocks for the entire filmstrip using a black marking pen and then tape the top and bottom leads to a table
and draw the entire sequence without moving it. In the long run this saves time
since students tend to slide the film before the ink is dry and a smear shows up.
The finished product might look something like this:

FOCUS
1ˢᵗ Grade -Naming-
🧍
PERSON
☆
STAR
🐟
FISH
☀
SUN

You should realize from looking at this filmstrip that not a
great amount of detail can be included using this technique. The topic and the storyboard will have to be
developed with this in mind.

To protect your finished filmstrip you should use a
clear plastic spray such as Spraylon or Krylon to insure
that the drawings will not be smeared. It is best to spray
the film outside since the fumes are strong. Hold the can
parallel to the filmstrip at a distance of one foot to keep
the spray from dripping or spotting on the filmstrip.

Once you have used up the damaged filmstrips, your local photographic
dealer should be willing to help you locate the cheapest means to buy the 35mm
nonphotographic film for this process. Buy in quantity if at all possible. If he
cannot locate a source, you may want to write to the following distributors for
exact costs:

Buhl Projector Company
60 Spruce Street
Paterson, N.J. 07501

Christy's
212 W. Magnolia Blvd.
Burbank, Calif. 91502

Film Makers
P.O. Box 593
Arcadia, Calif. 91006

If you desire more explanation of this procedure, you might want to invest in "Creating Your Own Filmstrip" produced by the International Film Bureau, Inc., 332 South Michigan Avenue, Chicago, Illinois 60604. The kit contains a 50-frame filmstrip in color with 33-1/3 rpm record ($29.50) or cassette tape ($31.50) and one box of twelve water-soluble oil colors, one number 3 brush, and thirteen 35mm blank filmstrips in cans. Additional paints, brushes, and 50, 100, or 1000 feet lengths of film are available.

SUPPLIERS OF EQUIPMENT AND SOFTWARE

Most school systems and public libraries have some arrangement with distributors of equipment for discounts below retail costs. If this is not the case, you will want to put the items out for bids once you have decided on particular equipment. This procedure should also be followed even if you personally want to buy the item—check a variety of stores and compare their prices *before* buying.

A good source to compare current prices is *The Audio-Visual Equipment Directory*, National Audio-Visual Association, Fairfax, Virginia (annual publication) for a listing of each item with specifications and price. The following are listed in this directory:

1.   copy stands

2.   tripods

3.   cassette tape recorders

4.   filmstrip projectors and/or viewers

Addresses for each equipment item are given at the end of the directory if you should desire additional information. Since cameras are not listed, you will need to contact your photographic stores for the particular SLR camera you decide to purchase. Most cameras will come with the standard features—f/1.7-1.8 50mm lens and built-in light meter. By talking with your local dealers you will quickly learn their preferences for durability and reliability. You might also want to get recommendations on a copy stand and tripod that will meet your specific needs.

35mm film and cassette tapes may be purchased at your camera store, photographic dealer, or discount stores. Be sure you ask for brand names, such as Kodak film or Ampex, Memorex, Sony, or 3M Scotch recording tape.

CHAPTER 3

SLIDE-TAPE PRESENTATIONS

Liberty Junior High School
Richardson, Texas

CHAPTER 3

SLIDE-TAPE PRESENTATIONS

INTRODUCTION

A note of caution from the beginning: don't tell anyone that you are considering a slide-tape presentation *until* you have made up your mind to do it. The main reason for this is that many individuals have tried this before either by themselves or with a group and have experienced numerous frustrations or have met with failure. Why? Very simply—lack of planning: "the cart was put before the horse!" This activity just like the others in this handbook *must* be storyboarded *before* you begin to draw, photograph, or tape. Even with proper planning you still must allot several hours per day—one hour for you and one for working with the students— over several weeks to complete the project.

Within the "sample format and evaluation for making a slide-tape presentation" on page 73 in this chapter, the media specialist mentions as one of the weaknesses of the activity: "very time consuming." However, I do not see this as a weakness *if* you take into account from the beginning that time *must* be spent for a *quality* production. If you find that you are taking 40 hours for such an activity, then something is wrong with the topic you have chosen to develop or with the organization of the procedures. Twelve to twenty hours should be long enough to zero in on a topic, storyboard, script, produce the art work, become familiar with the equipment, photograph the art, and tape the narration.

OBJECTIVES

To be able to develop a slide-tape presentation with or for a group of students, parents, or the community.

To be able to synchronize the tape with the slides to make a smooth presentation.

STRATEGIES

There are a wide variety of possibilities to interest students in producing a slide-tape presentation. I have found that perhaps one of the best ways is to invite a parent to show slides taken on a trip and explain each slide. This is especially effective if you are studying the topic in class and the students are somewhat familiar with the subject matter. If the parent does not object, you should tape the presentation and, possibly, borrow the slides.

As a group activity have the students view the slides again and listen to the tape. After each slide is explained, turn the tape recorder off and let the students condense the narration into one or two sentences. Have one student record the number of each slide and the suggested narration. When all slides have been viewed and a new narration written, ask the students to record their narration with an audible "ping" to indicate the change from one slide to another. Present your guest speaker with the cassette tape as a special "thank you" for his effort.

Another method that I have used is to buy commercial slides of my local area. I show these to students without narration; however, the students automatically respond with their own explanations of these familiar surroundings. The same procedure can be used as with the guest slide presentation.

These are only two ways to get students involved and thinking about making their own slide-tape production. You may wish to use either or both of the above and then ask them to suggest topics which they want to develop into a presentation. Also, you should ask them if they would be willing to show the presentation to other classes in the school and explain the steps they used to produce the finished product.

DEFINITION OF TERMS

The following terms are defined and illustrated in Chapter 2 "Making Filmstrips":

> 35mm SLR camera
> Close-up rings
> Cassette tape recorder
> Copy stand
> Tripod

Slide: 35mm film with one exposure each which has been mounted in a cardboard or plastic frame for easy handling and single viewing in a projector or hand viewer.

Light box or slide sorter: A clear plastic box with a light behind it used to view the slides individually and to place all of the slides of the presentation into proper sequence.

MATERIALS AND COSTS

You should expect the same costs for materials—equipment and software—that would be experienced with making and showing a filmstrip as discussed in Chapter 2; however, in order to view the presentation you will need a light box or slide sorter to help you place the slides in proper sequence and a slide projector to show the presentation.

Equipment

A. Camera

B. Close-up rings

C. Copy stand

D. Tripod

E. Cable release

F. Cassette tape recorder

G. Light box or slide sorter

A variety of light boxes or slide sorters are on the market. Surprisingly, they are sometimes hard to locate unless you can accurately describe over the phone what you want or unless you have a picture of the exact model desired. Your camera or photographic dealer may have some suggestions on where to go for this item. For your purpose, you do not need the most expensive slide sorter on the market. Currently, around $100 is what you should expect to pay.

H. Slide projector

There are a variety of slide projectors on the market today. Bell & Howell and Kodak are perhaps two of the leaders in the field; either one should give you excellent service. Depending upon the features you desire, such as manual or remote control focusing, remote slide control, zoom lens, automatic slide change at 5, 8, or 15 second intervals, you should expect to pay between $150-$250.

I.   Sound slide projectors with built-in screen

Singer, Kodak, and Bell & Howell all have similar models of the sound slide projectors with built-in screens. If you are going to invest in this item, it is wise if at all possible to buy the model that will allow you the most flexibility. For example, most brands include the following: cassette recorder-player with pulse and stop-pulse capabilities (allows you to place an inaudible sound on the tape for changing slides automatically or for stopping the program completely); individual viewing of slides; headphone jack which allows for individual or group listening; and even more recently, zoom capabilities on slides for close-up viewing or for use of 110 slides which are much smaller than the 35mm format and thus require magnification.

SUMMARY LIST OF ESTIMATED COSTS

Equipment

Item	Estimated Cost
camera	$200
close-up rings	20
copy stand	50
tripod	30
cable release	5
cassette tape recorder	150
light box	100
carousel slide projector	250
sound slide projector with built-in screen	450

A sound slide projector with built-in screen is not essential if you have a cassette tape recorder and a slide projector.

Software

cassette tapes	$1.50 each
film (20 exposures-36 exposures)	$2.50-4.00 each
processing	$2.00-3.50 each

Software prices will vary greatly depending on your shopping ability and sometimes the area in which you live.

PROCEDURE FOR PRODUCTION

In producing a slide-tape presentation some of the same items need to be considered as in making a filmstrip. Therefore, *before* you begin to read this section, review the following parts in chapter 2 (page 43ff.) and then return to this chapter for the specific procedures peculiar to making a slide-tape presentation:

1.   Art work

2.   Format of the pictures

3.   Content of the pictures

4.   Size of the pictures

5.   Helpful hints

6.   The 35mm camera: copy stand or tripod. In working with slides you have the option of shooting a variety of picture and/or subject sizes. Very simply this means that you can use the copy stand for taking the smaller pictures, then move the camera to the tripod for larger pictures or for photographing a subject, or you can hand hold the camera for shots of individuals, groups, buildings or scenes—all of which can easily be placed in sequence for the final presentation. For this reason, it is understandable why so many individuals prefer slide-tape presentations since this gives them the flexibility and freedom to rearrange or reshoot if one slide is not exactly what is needed.

If all of your slides for the topic you have storyboarded are to be original art by the students, for consistency and for viewing, you might want to consider masking each drawing. Using the dimensions shown below, produce a black mask made out of construction paper which you can lay over the finished picture on the copy stand:

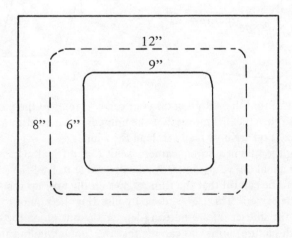

If students realize from the beginning that all of their work must be within this area, this feature will greatly enhance the quality of the finished presentation. Even if you desire to enlarge the drawings and move to a copy stand mask—multiply by two so you will have a mask 12"x18"—you still will have the same slide format that will fit into the rest of your program.

7.   Film for the 35mm camera: choice and loading. Slides may be made using a variety of film: Kodachrome II, Kodachrome X, or Ektachrome 64 or 160. If you are going to be working with a copy stand or a tripod *inside* using artificial light, then Ektachrome 160 tungsten film is best. However, if you are going to use a copy stand or tripod *outside* or are going to be taking shots of buildings and/or scenery using natural light, then you may use any of the film listed above. Ektachrome 64 daylight film or Kodachrome X will give you good results for the copy stand or tripod if you are using sunlight.

Once you have selected the film, make sure you notice on the side of the box the ASA setting. For example, the box will have one of the following markings:

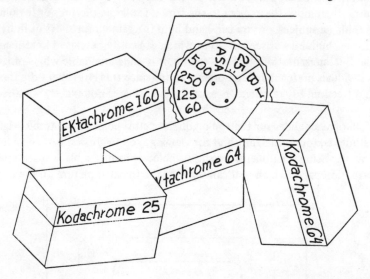

You will want to find the ASA dial on your camera (refer to the picture above) and pull up. Notice that the dial moves. Set the number on the dial to match the number on the box. You are now ready to load the film.

Loading the film in a 35mm camera is not that difficult. Once you have scanned the manual on your camera, you will be able to load the film very quickly. You do need to be careful that the film catches on the take-up spool before closing the back of the camera. This can be done by inserting the film onto the spool and then tripping the shutter release button (depress the button on top of the camera for taking each picture) until you can see that the film is winding around the take-up spool. Close the camera and check the counter to see if it registers on number 1. I prefer to waste a few slides with the lens cover on the camera to make sure the film is in place for taking the first actual slide of the presentation.

8. Photographing the pictures

    a. Camera on copy stand. When using a copy stand for taking slides, you do not have to worry about the direction of the picture or whether you are taking it upside down or not. Once the slides are processed, you have complete control over the way you wish the scene to be viewed or the direction a word will be read.

    If a mask is not used to cover the pictures you are copying, place a black piece of construction paper on the base of the copy stand and roll tape underneath the paper to hold it steady so it will not move as you position the picture.

    Place the camera on the screw mount and adjust the bracket until the picture can be viewed through the lens and brought into proper focus. If you have kept the pictures within the 6"x9" format, you should experience no difficulty with focusing and framing the masked or unmasked picture. If the picture is masked, you might want to allow a slight margin of the mask to show on all the slides; however, if not masked, you might wish to lightly mark the edges of the placement of your first picture so that the remaining pictures can quickly be located on the same space. A slight margin is also advisable here so that you have a type of frame around the drawing to be photographed.

    Once your picture is focused and framed, you will need to adjust the lights of the copy stand so that there are no "hot spots" on the pictures. The light shining from the spotlights should be evenly distributed so that when you look through the lens, parts of the picture are *not* lighter or are completely washed out by the bright lights. Be careful to check this with each picture.

    When the lights are positioned, you need to set the light meter on your camera. Most cameras purchased today have a built-in meter which registers the correct amount of light. Again, knowing your camera and how your particular meter works in advance will insure the best results. For most cameras when you look through the lens you will see a needle to the right of the frame which will move if you place your hand in front of the camera. You will need to match up the circle over top of the needle in order to have a correct exposure.

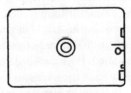

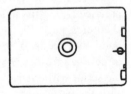

Incorrect exposure   Correct exposure

If you experience difficulty with this step, you will want to check with your camera dealer to see if your meter is registering correctly or if the battery which supplies the energy for the meter to operate is low or is not working.

When the meter is in correct alignment, you are ready to take your slides. Remember that if for some reason you move the camera while taking a picture or if you are unsure of the focus, you can always take another picture once you have repositioned or readjusted the camera. For best results when using a camera mounted on a copy stand, you will want to use a cable release. This keeps you from jarring the camera once it is set for the shot.

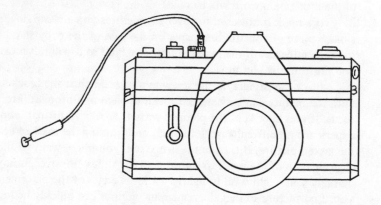

Cable release attached to 35mm camera

b. Camera on a tripod. The same procedure can be used with a tripod as with the copy stand. The only major difference is mounting the pictures. If you use the 12"x18" mask, you will want to tape it to a blackboard or staple it to a bulletin board and leave the top open to slide the pictures into place. If you use a black or gray piece of construction paper as a background, again you will want to stabilize it so that the pictures can be taped or pinned to the background. With a tripod you have a wider range of possibilities to include in your pictures. So long as you do not go any smaller than 6"x9"—the same size as the copy stand format—you can use your tripod to move in closer or move as far away as necessary. *Suggestion*: when making a slide presentation, if possible, take two exposures of each print so that you will have a duplicate of each picture.

9. Taping the narration. Once the filming is completed, you will want to practice taping the narration. The same procedure is used as described in chapter 2, page 49, for taping the narration of a filmstrip. One important point that needs to be mentioned is that additional time between slides needs to be given for the *viewer* to focus on the visual. If you record straight through the script without pauses, you will find that once the slides are synchronized with the narration, it becomes extremely difficult to view the information in

the visual, much less change from one slide to another and also listen to the spoken words. Practice taping the script and then combining the two—words with visual—will help you determine the total effectiveness of the presentation.

If you do not have the means to place an inaudible pulse on your tape once it is recorded, you will need to allow for an audible "ping" to indicate the change from one slide to another. This can be done by having a student stand next to the microphone while taping and on cue from you or another student following the narration lightly tap a triangle or crystal glass.

10.   Placement of slides in the projector. Most individuals forget that a projector reverses the slide image. Very simply this means that slides in your production must be placed upside down and backwards in order to be viewed correctly. To insure that you have them correctly placed, it is a good idea while your slides are still on the light box—in proper sequence and *exactly* as you would expect them to appear on the screen—that you mark the lower left-hand corner with a small dot using a felt-tip permanent ink pen. Turn the slides upside down and then number them #1, #2, and so on. The slides may then be placed into the slide tray. *Always* check placement of these slides by projecting them onto a screen *before* the showing.

11.   The showing.

12.   Copying the slide-tape presentation.

Items 11 and 12 are described in detail in chapter 2, page 49. Copying the slides of the presentation is usually much easier than copying a filmstrip. Most photographic stores supply this service at a cost of between $0.30-$0.35 per slide. Again, if you realize in the beginning that you want a duplicate copy of the presentation, it is less expensive to make the second slide at the same time you are shooting the originals.

SAMPLE FORMAT AND EVALUATION FOR MAKING A SLIDE-TAPE PRESENTATION

The following slide-tape presentation was developed by a high school media specialist working with students in a special area—environmental science. Notice that the class was divided into three groups which allowed each student to contribute in part to the total production. Documentation of the group, the specific objective, references, procedure, strengths/weaknesses and the actual script are most helpful to have on file for future reference in case you want to share your experience with others who wish to see at a glance what is involved.

ENVIRONMENTAL AWARENESS

GROUP: Twenty-five students in an Environmental Science class

OBJECTIVE: To determine and examine causes for the decline in the
                    environmental quality of our earth and the progress
                    being made in improving it.

REFERENCES: National Geographic Society, ed. *Wilderness U.S.A.* 3rd
                    ed. Washington, D.C.: National Geographic Society, 1975.

                    Reader's Digest Association, Inc. *Our Magnificent Wild-
                    life: How to Enjoy and Preserve It.* Pleasantville, N.Y.:
                    Reader's Digest Association, Inc., 1975.

PERIODICALS USED: *National Geographic*
                    National Wildlife
                    Natural History
                    Newsweek

PROCEDURE: Divided class into three groups:

                    Group I: responsible for research, outlining and
                                  script writing

                    Group II: responsible for selecting pictures and
                                  photographing

                    Group III: responsible for production (putting the
                                  program together, synchronizing slide/
                                  sound presentation)

STRENGTHS: 1. Eager participation by all; afforded even the most shy
                    student an opportunity to participate in some successful
                    manner.

                    2. Provided opportunity for extensive research in books
                    and periodicals and into local environmental conditions.

                    3. Developed environmental awareness on a local and
                    personal level.

                    4. Afforded students an opportunity to use and become
                    skillful in a variety of media and equipment.

WEAKNESSES: 1. Selected too broad a subject (one area might have been better; i.e., air pollution).

2. Very time consuming; approximately twelve hours were needed from outset to conclusion. Some of this was used in becoming familiar with equipment. Group III found that synchronizing slide/sound to be frustrating at first. BUT WE ALL LEARNED!

SCRIPT:

ENVIRONMENTAL AWARENESS

NARRATION

SLIDE #

1.   Environment is more than a big word.

2.   Our environment is a challenge to modern society and our beautiful earth is being eroded by many forces.

3.   Our forefathers

4.   found a land of great beauty and

5.   bountiful in productivity.

6.   As many pioneers exhausted their farmlands, they moved westward to more fertile fields abandoning their poor lands to the ravages of nature. The abundance of land contributed to waste.

7.   The population explosion and

8.   man's technology have hastened the decline of our environment.

9.   People (pause)

10. products (pause)

11. and technology are contributing factors to pollution.

12. Visual and noise pollution,

13. technological pollution,

14. careless removal of top soil,

15. strip mining,

(Continued on page 74)

16. acid runoff from coal mining,

17. soil erosion,

18. abuse of timberlands,

19. industrial dumps, and

20. urban wastes are

21. smothering humanity.

22. Man is beginning to become aware of his environmental quality. He is taking steps to reclaim and protect his environment as in

23. soil conservation,

24. (pause)

25. nature pathways

26. use of solar energy,

27. energy conservation

28. even returnable bottles in an effort to

29. restore beauty and

30. bounty

31. to our world.

—Eloise Reams

ANNOTATED BIBLIOGRAPHY

Boniol, John D. "Making Slides Without Cameras," *School Library Journal* (April 1975):36.
Three methods are explained in making slides without cameras: draw-on/ paint-on slides; laminating film or contact paper slides; and scratch-on slides. Materials needed and helpful hints in producing the slides are also given.

Brown, James W., and Richard B. Lewis, Eds. *AV Instructional Technology Manual for Independent Study.* 5th ed. New York: McGraw-Hill, 1977, pp. 55-56, 59-62.
Methods of copying materials, storyboarding, developing one-screen and multi-screen, multi-media presentations are covered. Illustrated.

Brown, James W., Richard B. Lewis, and Fred F. Harcleroad. *A V Instruction: Technology, Media, and Methods.* 5th ed. New York: McGraw-Hill, 1977, pp. 149-68, 188-89.
Authors discuss informal and structured photography, production formats, presentation techniques, organizing your slide collection, and teaching with slides. Illustrated.

Kemp, Jerrold F. *Planning and Producing Audiovisual Materials.* 3rd ed. New York: Thomas Y. Crowell, 1975, pp. 171-83.
In one chapter, "Slide Series," the author explains the process of taking pictures, processing film, editing slides, preparing slides for use, duplicating and filing slides, selecting a projector, techniques of projection, and use of the series. Illustrated.

McBride, Otis. "Local Production with 35mm Photography," *School Libraries* (Winter 1971):25-27.
Basic information regarding the camera and film is given. Details are explained, such as meanings of "rangefinder," "exposure meter," "viewfinder," "focus," "shutter," and "stops." Sequencing pictures for photographing is diagrammed. Illustrated.

Orgren, Carl F. "Production of Slide-Tape Programs," *Unabashed Librarian* (Summer 1975):25-28.
A detailed article which takes a step-by-step approach to the process involved in putting a slide/tape presentation together. Choice of medium, purpose, planning, technical considerations and equipment needs are presented.

Palmer, Millicent. "Creating Slide-Tape Library Instruction: The Librarian's Role," *Drexel Library Quarterly* (July 1972):251-67.
A detailed narrative on the steps taken to produce slide-tape library instruction. Information on the equipment, planning the narration and visuals, sample script, and "putting it all together" are explained.

Ryan, Mack. "Preparing a Slide-Tape Program: A Step-by-Step Approach; Part I/ Part II," *Audiovisual Instruction* (Sept. 1975/Nov. 1975):36-38/36-38.
A two-part article which takes a step-by-step approach to explaining the details necessary to produce a quality slide/tape presentation. A number of helpful hints are given in organizing and selecting visuals and in the cost of basic equipment to film and tape the program.

Turner, Philip M. *Handbook for In-school Media Personnel.* Green Bay, WI: PLT Publications, 1975, pp. 40-43.
Equipment and recommendations for taking slides are covered.

Wagner, Betty J., and E. Arthur Stunard. *Making and Using Inexpensive Classroom Media.* Palo Alto, Calif.: Education Today Co., 1975, pp. 35-38.
Suggestions on how to purchase slides, add narration and music are given

"Slide-making without a camera" and "cassette recordings" are also covered. Illustrated.

Wittich, Walter S., and Charles F. Schuller. *Instructional Technology: Its Nature and Use.* 5th ed. New York: Harper and Row, 1973, pp. 394-445. Examines still projection, types and equipment used. Briefly covers specialized slide applications.

ADDITIONAL SOURCES OF INFORMATION

Producing Slides and Filmstrips. Write to: Eastman Kodak Co., 343 State Street, Rochester, NY 14650.

Cyr, Don. "How to Turn Kids On to Photography," *Popular Photography* (July 1975-April 1976). (Ten detailed projects beginning July 1975.)

Cooper, Douglas, and Sharon Cooper. "Kids, Cameras, and Communication," *Media Spectrum* (1975):5-7, 22.

Dayton, Deane. "Making Title Slides with High Contrast Film," *Audiovisual Instruction* (April 1977):33-36; (May 1977):39-41.

Jenkins, David. "Multiple Image Slides," *Audiovisual Instruction* (Jan. 1977):41-43.

SUGGESTIONS FOR FOLLOW-UP ACTIVITIES

Refer to the same section in chapter 2, numbers 1-5. Some of the same suggested activities for producing a filmstrip could apply to the slide-tape presentation.

Additional activities you might wish to consider are:

1.   Once you have your slides in *exactly* the right sequence, you might want to consider making the presentation into a filmstrip.

For the best results you must send the originals; however, make sure you have a copy of all the slides in case they are lost in transport. You should write for general information *first* to one of the following addresses:

Lowell T. Nerge
11941 Jefferson Street N.E.
Minneapolis, Minn. 55434
(ask for "Filmstrips from 35mm Slide
   Series")

Stokes Slide Services
7000 Cameron Road
Austin, Texas 78752
(ask for "Price List")

After reading their brochures, make sure you *follow the instructions to the letter* to save them and you time.

A copy or *copies* may be made for the library/media center or for wider distribution throughout your school district. If you produce a slide-tape presentation which is most unusual or which you feel is outstanding for the curriculum, you might even consider sending a copy to a publisher of multi-media materials for publication.

2.   Now that you have mastered the 35mm camera, you should try using a Kodak Ektagraphic Visualmaker which comes with an instamatic camera; cost $175 or $195 depending on the size. Two sizes are available: 3"x3" and 8"x8"—which denotes the size of the area which can be copied. Younger and older students will have *no* problem using this piece of equipment on their own.

Photographs taken on trips, old postcards stuck away in boxes, or pictures from magazines and newspapers that a student wants to use in a report may all be copied using the Ektagraphic and made into slides as long as they are no larger than the area indicated above. If smaller, you may want to use colored construction paper for a frame to lay the picture on or to give variety to your visuals.

For additional information write to Eastman Kodak Company, 343 State Street, Rochester, New York 14650.

3.   Your students might want to try their hand at making their own slides; three simple methods may be used:
    a.   drawing or painting on clear transparency film or on non-photographic film. This may be obtained from your photographic dealer or ordered from a variety of sources, such as Seal, Inc., 550 Spring St., Naugatuck, Connecticut 06770; 3M Company, Visual Products Division, 3M Center, St. Paul, Minnesota 55101; Scott Education Division, 104 Lower Westfield Road, Holyoke, Massachusetts 01040.

Transparency marking pens, water-soluble oil colors, food coloring, or colored plastic adhesive cut in a variety of shapes may be used to achieve an endless variety of effects.

If you use transparency film, it will have to be cut using scissors or a paper cutter to the proper size for placing in a slide mount. If you use nonphotographic 35mm film, you can mark off the areas for the students to work within and then cut each frame for mounting. To protect the visual drawn on either of these films, you should spray it with a clear acrylic spray—Krylon or Spraylon—which places a plastic film over the drawing and will keep it from smearing.

    b.   lifting clay based pictures using clear contact paper or laminating film: 1) place the adhesive side of the contact paper against the clay base picture (most magazines are clay base, for example, *National Geographic*) and burnish the top of the contact paper with a coin or smooth plastic spatula; rub the surface until a consistent bond between picture and contact paper is apparent; soak the combination in warm soapy water until the picture can be peeled off the back and all of the white filmy residue wiped off with a cotton swab or ball (the original picture—now translucent, should remain on the contact paper); allow time for drying and either cover the once adhesive side with clear plastic or use a clear floor wax to paint the back of the picture. 2) If you are familiar with laminating film, you may want to have your students place the dull side of the film against the clay base picture and using a dry mount press set at around 275°F, a tacking iron set on HIGH, or a regular iron *without* steam set on "cotton," sandwich the film placed on the picture inbetween clean newsprint or butcher paper and heat the film until it adheres completely to the picture (after you have tried this a few times you will learn the length of time required for the film to adhere using each method); the same steps are then taken as explained when using the contact paper.

c.   scratching on unprocessed 35mm film or on clear transparency film coated with water-soluble oil paints, food coloring, or a variety of marking pens can produce most unusual effects; if unprocessed film is used, make sure you scratch with an X-ACTO® knife, single-edged razor blade or other sharp object on the dull side of the film being careful not to cut into it; to add color you can paint the scratched design with colored marking pens or food coloring; if clear film is used, either side may be painted but be sure to make the color cover consistent and heavy enough so that it can be scratched away from the surface.

If you decide to make your own slides, then you will need to purchase slide mounts—either plastic which can be reused or cardboard which when heated and sealed may *not* be reused—for between $3.00-$4.00 per 100. These are commonly known as "ready mounts."

For additional information on any of the above, see John Boniol's "Making Slides Without Cameras" referenced in the bibliography of this chapter (page 74).

SUPPLIERS OF EQUIPMENT AND SOFTWARE

The following equipment items are listed in *The Audio-Visual Equipment Directory*, National Audio-Visual Association (NAVA), Fairfax, Virginia (annual publication):

copy stands
tripods
cassette tape players
carousel projectors
sound slide projectors with built-in screens
dry mount presses
Ektagraphic slide copiers

On all of these items, remember that the quoted price is list (recommended retail selling price) and by either placing any item on competitive bidding or by comparing local dealer prices, you can significantly reduce the cost.

Since 35mm cameras are not listed, you will have to talk with your local camera shop or photographic dealer regarding the most reliable and durable camera for use by students. Again, compare prices and choose not only the best camera but also check out the shop or dealer to help you determine the kind of service he will give if something happens to the camera and it requires maintenance.

Light boxes are also not included in the NAVA catalog. If your camera shop or photographic supplier cannot give you the names of any dealers, you may want to write for information on their models and costs to:

Knox Manufacturing Company
Acculight Division
111 Spruce Street
Wood Dale, Illinois 60191

Matrix/Leedal, Inc.
2929 S. Halsted Street
Chicago, Illinois 60608

Software items such as 35mm film and cassette tape cartridges should be brand names: Kodak film and Ampex, Memorex, Sony or 3M Scotch for cassette tapes. By buying brand names which perhaps are a little more expensive, you will insure the quality of the finished production and also the durability.

CHAPTER 4

SUPER 8mm MOVIE PRODUCTIONS

Denton High School
Denton, Texas

CHAPTER 4

SUPER 8mm MOVIE PRODUCTIONS

INTRODUCTION

There is an abundance of information regarding making super 8mm movies—turn to the end of this chapter to the "Annotated Bibliography" and you will see only a few of the print and nonprint items on the successful integration of motion pictures into the curriculum. Why? What are some of the possible reasons for this overwhelming appeal?

Motion pictures, especially those in the 16mm format, have been with us for some time now. With the advent of regular 8mm and then super 8mm, the expense of equipment and film has been greatly reduced—reduced to such an extent that it is rather commonplace for families to own the majority of equipment in the 8mm line for taking and showing home movies. If this format is available in the home, students have been exposed to it *before* its inclusion in the schools. It is not surprising, therefore, that students are more comfortable with using the medium than the teacher.

Another possible reason for the appeal of the 8mm format is that once the basics are learned either in a group experience or by an individual, there is an endless variety of ways to manipulate the medium to achieve the desired effect. For example, once the group has planned and produced the live action presentation discussed in the book, they may want to continue their investigation into other areas such as animation and pixilation. From my point of view, it would be a mistake for anyone or any group to start off with either one of these last two techniques *until* they have planned in detail the live action movie. Once they have learned the steps in this production, then they should investigate other methods by reading and/or viewing some of the suggested print/nonprint materials listed in the bibliography.

OBJECTIVE

To learn how to produce a super 8mm live action movie.

STRATEGIES

Perhaps one of the best ways to get your students totally involved in the super 8mm format is to ask them to bring one of their "home movies" to class. Show a few of these to the class and ask for comments. After about the third movie, students will begin to recognize that all of the movies viewed share one common element—aimless shooting. This is typical of "home movies"; there is very little rhyme or reason for the sequence of events included. These movies are not planned; they happen at birthdays, during the holidays, or when something "cute" happens and the camera is grabbed.

Once the students recognize this common element—and they will even if you don't bring it up, show them a single-concept super 8mm movie. The contrast should be both shocking and evident to any viewer. There is no aimless shooting in the single-concept movie. Every sequence has been well-planned *in advance* before the film was loaded and the camera moved into place. The lighting is exactly enough and the movement from one scene to another is clear and distinct.

By all means do not let the contrast between the two different types of movies scare your students. I have had such comments as "We'll never be able to do a movie like that single-concept!" Yes, they will—if they storyboard, research, plan, and rehearse in advance. Careful step-by-step planning, just as in the other areas discussed in this book, is the key to success.

DEFINITION OF TERMS

8mm film: Refers to the width of a single frame of film; two sizes presently exist—standard 8mm and super 8mm; notice the difference not only in frame size between standard and super 8mm, but also the decrease in the size of the sprocket holes on the super versus the standard; super 8mm is on the same ratio (3:4) as 16mm film which makes it possible to copy from 16mm to 8mm without losing any of the picture.

8mm camera: A camera which has the capability of recording motion either  continuous or frame-by-frame onto 8mm film; most cameras sold today are super 8mm and use a 50-foot cartridge film which reproduces live action at 18 frames per second; some cameras have the capabilities of single-frame exposure and variation of number of frames per second for fast or slow motion which is useful for animation and pixilation.

8mm projector: A projector which accepts and projects 8mm film.  A variety of projectors are available for purchase. Most reel-to-reel projectors allow for conversion from standard 8mm to super 8mm simply by flipping a switch. There are four major types:
1. silent reel-to-reel
2. sound reel-to-reel

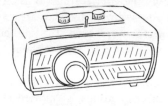

3. silent cartridge load
4. sound cartridge load

Live action: A process of recording on film with the use of a motion picture camera continuous action as it occurs in real life and as it will be replayed for viewing; the normal shooting speed for live action is 18 frames per second and when shown on the projector, the same frame-per-second count is maintained.

Animation: A process of recording on film with the use of a motion picture camera, single frame or two to five frame sequences at a much slower pace than the film will eventually be viewed. Using this technique, inanimate objects appear to achieve motion simply by taking a few frames at a time with the camera and then slightly moving the object; when the film is projected at 18 frames per second, the object appears to move.

Pixilation: A process of recording on film with the use of a motion picture camera, single-frame shots of live action. With pixilation the subject moves only slightly between frame shots. Using this technique, impossible tasks may "seemingly" be accomplished with ease, such as a person driving down a street without a car.

Cable release: An attachment to the camera which will allow you to trip the shutter one frame at a time for animation or pixilation.

MATERIALS AND COSTS

Your investment in hardware will be the greatest initial expense in making super 8mm movies. Depending on your tastes and most certainly your budget, silent to sound cameras may run from $150 to $2000. For the purpose of this activity and the others listed under "Suggestions for Follow-Up Activities," your best buy would be a sound camera with a zoom lens, reflex (through the lens) viewing, capability for ASA 160 film using only existing light, remote control and single frame capabilities. For such a camera you should expect to pay around $350. If you opt to buy the camera *without* sound and desire the *same* features as listed above, you can cut your price to $200. Brands that you will want to check are Bolex, GAF, Eumig, Bell & Howell, and Kodak. Projectors for viewing the finished project also have a wide range of prices: from $650 with sound to $100 without sound, again depending upon the make and sophistication you desire. The same brands should be consulted as in the cameras. One of the Kodak projectors has a unique feature which would be appealing for use with small groups—a "moviedeck" which is a built-in small screen attached to the projector. A minimum expenditure is $300.

The cost of editing equipment—a viewer and splicer—is most reasonable. For class use both items may be purchased as a unit for around $35.

Film prices will vary widely. SHOP first before buying. Discount stores are usually much cheaper. At times you can save as much as one dollar on the film and the same on processing if you are willing to mail the film off and wait a few days.

SUMMARY LIST OF ESTIMATED COSTS

Equipment

Item	Estimated Cost
camera:	
sound	$350
silent	200
projector:	
sound	350-550
silent	100
editing equipment	35

Software

super 8mm film:	
ASA 40 (Kodachrome):	
silent	$3.00
sound	6.00
ASA 160 (Ecktachrome):	
silent	3.50
sound	6.50
processing (per 50' cartridge)	2.00
splicing tape (20 units)	.60

PROCEDURE FOR PRODUCTION

Live action photography is perhaps the safest way for you and your students to begin with super 8mm moviemaking. If you are to avoid cutting out mistakes or rearranging shots taken out of sequence, careful storyboarding and at least two practice sessions using the storyboard developed into a script with an estimate of the time to be taken for each shot and the camera positions, such as "long shot" or "close-up," is essential. Beware not to overemphasize the importance of "practice makes perfect." Unlike the filmstrip, if a mistake is made while shooting, it can be taken out with editing equipment without having to start over. Students should enjoy the experience of working with all of the nonprint techniques; however, they should also realize that money is involved when the camera and film are combined.

The following steps might be followed to insure a smooth first encounter with the super 8mm format:

1.   Once the students have decided on a topic, sketched the storyboard, researched the topic, expanded the storyboard and written the script, they are ready to run through the shooting with all of the equipment *minus* the film. Each sequence must be timed as accurately as possible. Record this time using either a stop watch or the second hand on a wrist watch. Write down each estimate under the picture on the left-hand side of the script. Also, if the camera is to be moved during the sequence, you will need to write down next to the time what the shot is supposed to be: "close-up" (c.s.), "medium shot" (m.s.), "long shot" (l.s.), or "move from l.s.———c.s." Students may have already written these instructions down on their first or second draft of their storyboard, but the only way they will know how this looks is to practice with the camera.

2.   To avoid a jerky movie, it is best to place the camera on a tripod. Most tripods are equipped so that they may be raised or lowered, elevated or tilted up or down, or moved smoothly from left to right and back. If a shot requires more motion on the part of the camera than is allowed with the tripod, the shot can be taken holding the camera, as long as the individual rests his elbows against his chest and moves slowly while taking the shot.

3.   The film that you choose to use in your camera will depend on the amount of available light falling on the subject you are filming. If you are filming outside, you can probably use Kodachrome film with an ASA of 40. This would also apply for use inside *if* some type of extra lighting is available beyond existing ceiling lights. If shooting inside, be careful *not* to use fluorescent lights, since these lights tend to discolor your film. (I have had the bad experience of having an entire roll taken under fluorescent lights returned with a blue haze surrounding everything.) The best film to use with inside filming is Ektachrome film with an ASA of 160. With this film you may use existing natural light. If you use flood lights, you will want to buy Ektachrome *tungsten* film.

      Once your film is loaded, you will want to check to see if you have enough light available for filming by using the light meter normally built into the camera or by checking with a hand light meter. Again, the instruction manual to your camera should provide an explanation for checking on sufficient lighting.

4.   If your camera is equipped with "special effects" capabilities such as dissolve or fade from one scene to another, students might want to incorporate these into the script; however, they should be cautious of overusing these effects. Overuse tends to take away from the final production. Your audience will tend to look more at the special effects than the intended message. Even

if the camera does not have these capabilities, you can simulate some of them by gradually moving a piece of black construction paper in front of the lens of the camera at the end of a scene and removing it at the beginning of the next scene. Your students will want to try more special effects as they become comfortable with the medium.

5.   Continuity from shot to shot is another important consideration when beginning to use super 8mm for the first time. Students need to be reminded that each shot should be logically tied into the next one. Some adjustment of the script may be made when the practice sessions begin. It would be very tiring for any viewer to watch a film which constantly moves with every different shot from close-up to long to close-up, *et cetera*. There should be a smooth flow from one scene to another; from a long shot to a close-up. There should be a *reason* for moving in close or moving farther away.

6.   Most projectors display super 8mm film at 18 frames per second. You need to match up the frames that you are taking per second on your camera with a projector you plan on using (check your manual). Most inexpensive super 8mm cameras have the frames-per-second pre-set with adjustments to this impossible. However, once your students have made the first film, they may—if the variation in speed is available—want to consider a slow motion film (taken at 24 frames per second [fps] and played back at 18 fps on the projector) or a faster motion film (taken at 12 fps and played back at 18 fps on the projector).

7.   Editing (or removing) unwanted scenes or scenes incorrectly exposed is not that difficult. Once the film has been processed and is returned, view it from beginning to end noting any problem areas. Editing is completed by using a viewer, a splicer which cuts the film, and splicing tape as shown below.

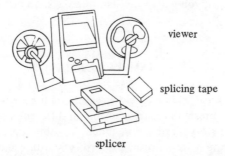

viewer

splicing tape

splicer

Most editing units include all three items with a visual instructional booklet for the step-by-step procedure. This equipment is always handy to have even if you do not need it for the first movie.

8.   If you are fortunate enough to be able to buy or already own a sound camera and projector, then by all means produce sound movies. If, on the other hand, you are restricted to using the silent camera-projector system, do not feel that the task is impossible to synchronize the picture with a cassette tape recording; however, do not think that the task will be easy either. If you do not have sound recording capabilities built in, it is best to incorporate written title cards between scenes which will help to bridge the train of thought and make for transitions which are easily understood. View a single-concept movie, and you will see what I mean. Even if this is done, suitable musical accompaniment recorded on a cassette helps when showing the movie.

If students are determined to attempt a synchronization between the visual display and the spoken narration, do not discourage this as long as they know the problems they are going to encounter. The spoken narration needs to be slightly shorter than the viewing time for each scene. A cue must be placed on the film, such as a red dot of at least 5 seconds duration so that the viewer will know when to roll the recorded cassette tape. The actual recording must be made separate from the projector, such as through a window with the projector on one side and the narrator on the other, so that the sound from the projector is not recorded. Experimentation is the only means to judge the success or failure of this method.

Another method that should not be overlooked if you cannot afford a sound camera but own a sound projector is the possibility of sending your completed movie off to a processing center where a magnetic sound strip is added. When returned, you view your film and record the sound narration or music directly onto the film.

Making copies of your original movie are expensive but not impossible. Most photographic dealers will charge around 24 cents a foot or $12.00 for a 50' roll of film. If you have a movie that you know will be viewed a number of times by individuals and groups, you will more than likely want a copy to protect your original print.

SAMPLE FORMAT

The sample format included below represents the steps taken by two post-graduate students interested in making a film on different weightlifting techniques. If the entire original storyboard was included, it would represent three to four pages of this book. Once the fellows finished the storyboarding and scripting, they realized what a monumental task they had undertaken and as a result of this realization, found it necessary to include only the essentials. Three rolls (150 feet) of film were shot which were later edited down to around 100 feet or 7 minutes in length. The exercise, although costly from my point of view, was well worth it, since it reinforced my stand that choice of topic is critical when working with super 8mm movies—the simpler the better, especially the first time around.

WEIGHTLIFTING

OBJECTIVE: To show weight lifts which will develop different muscles of the body.

RESOURCES: *Dictionary of Sports*; Ryan's *Weight Training*; *Sports Illustrated*; personal interviews.

PROCEDURE: Step 1—Once we decided on a topic, we both did research using the resources listed above. We also talked with the Physical Education teacher, Mr. Bruce. He gave us permission to use the weightlifting room for filming and also some names of students that he thought might be subjects for the movie.

Step 2—Next we listed all of the different lifts we wanted to show. Since there were 17 lifts, we thought that it would be best if we took only two from each area. This cut the number of different shots down to eight. Using this list we arranged them in sequence so we could easily move from one shot to the next. We also decided to attempt a cassette tape to accompany the movie.

Step 3—A storyboard of 20 cards was drawn up showing each lift with a brief description of the sketch. These were placed on the bulletin board to check for sequencing. The person we chose to be in the movie looked over the cards and gave us an estimate of the amount of time for each lift. These times were recorded on the cards and the total was 6 minutes.

Step 4—Using the storyboard cards for guidance, we returned to our resources and read about each lift. The information was shortened to a description which when read aloud lasted slightly under the time estimated to visualize the lift.

Step 5—Our filming plans were written out in script form with a brief sketch on the left side of the page and the narration on the right.

Step 6—Before the filming began, we ran through the sequence entirely two times with one of us reading the narration while the other ran the camera without film. The location of the camera for long shots and close-ups was noted the first time and checked the second time. It took two hours to complete this step.

PROCEDURE (cont'd):   Step 7—Filming of the actual movie only took 45 minutes. Only twice did we have to re-take a shot because the weightlifter dropped the weights.

Step 8—When the film had been processed, the two mistakes were edited out and reviewed.

Step 9—A cassette tape recording was made to go with the film to explain the lifts. The projector and movie were placed in a small viewing room with a window. One of us looked through the window and made the recording on the other side as the film was shown.

Step 10—The movie was shown to the faculty and student body. It was difficult to keep the tape recording and movie in sync all the time.

—Buddie Taylor
—Scott Wilder

SUGGESTIONS FOR FOLLOW-UP ACTIVITIES

1.   Once your students have successfully produced a live action super 8mm movie, they are bound to want to try other techniques. The next step is an attempt with animation. Decide on an inanimate object, such as a rock, torn paper, clay, or cut out drawings which you want to "come to life." Even with the first few attempts, students might want to do research on a particular process, such as the development of a flower from a seed to full growth and animate this. If taken step-by-step, the animation of any such process can be easy—if you remember to storyboard and check the sequencing *before* beginning.

Although filming is much easier and more successful if you have single frame capabilities (this allows you to take one frame at a time and then *slightly* move the object), you should not hesitate to try this with a regular super 8mm camera without this capability. Short flickers on the trigger of the camera will allow you to achieve the same effect. Another helpful attachment for your camera for animation is a cable release which serves as a trigger to set the film in motion. This keeps your hands off the camera and thus prevents you from possibly jarring the entire camera (page 93).

When shooting an animated movie, you will need either a copy stand or tripod to hold the camera steady.

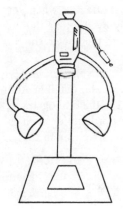

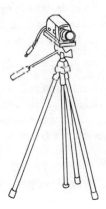

Copy stand set up   Tripod set up

The same copy stand (cost approximately $50) and/or tripod (cost approximately $30) as discussed in chapters 2 and 3 with 35mm cameras may be used with the movie camera.

You may greatly decrease the cost of your film if you use natural light to illuminate the objects you wish to animate. Under these conditions try Kodachrome film. If you are forced to use existing light of low illumination, you will have to use Ecktachrome film. If you use spot lights with the Ecktachrome, be sure to buy tungsten film. Most cameras either have an automatic electric eye which will adjust the light falling onto the film or a built-in light meter similar to the 35mm camera which allows you to adjust the lens opening until enough light is available. Familiarity with your camera and reading the instruction booklet will quickly answer these questions.

Once you have loaded the film, mount the camera on the copy stand or tripod. One person should be in charge of the script sequence, one in charge of the camera and another should work with moving the objects. Check the lighting, the focus, and begin.

For the first attempt you may want to try something *very* simple, such as a dot moving across the page or a series of dots in motion. Expose *three* frames—one sudden burst on the trigger or three clicks with the cable release—per motion. With the first roll of film (approximately three minutes 20 seconds in length) you might want to include three one-minute animated series for experimentation to check for proper light exposure and to see if your movements are too fast.

2.   Another technique your students will want to try is pixilation. Using this live-action technique, individuals can accomplish seemingly impossible tasks, such as driving down a road without a motorcycle. To achieve this effect, the camera needs to be placed on a tripod so that the only thing moving will be the subject. Expose *three* frames per movement and then allow the person to move slightly. As the person begins to move out of view, reposition the tripod for another series of shots. This technique is effective when you wish someone to magically appear or disappear simply by stopping the camera, having the person walk into or out of place and then begin the film again.

Both animation and pixilation are explained in much greater detail in Andrew and Mark Hobson's *Film Animation as a Hobby*, referenced in the bibliography. Also, it might be meaningful for your class to view a student production such as "How to Animate a Gingerbread Boy" or "Neighbors," also referenced in the bibliography.

3.   A final activity which is relatively inexpensive, once you own a projector and some super 8mm film, is drawing directly onto the film with permanent felt-tip pens or paints. If your students have pieces of processed film or if you can find a local dealer that will sell or give you unwanted super 8mm film, you can clean it with a solution of one cup bleach to one sink of warm water. Rinse the film and let dry. Use felt-tip pens that give bold colors or paints that are translucent and that will not crack when run through a projector. *NEVER* use crayons or grease pencils since they will gum up your projector. To protect your drawing, you might want to cover the sprocket holes with a piece of paper after taping the two ends of the film down on cardboard and spray a light film of clear acrylic plastic, such as Krylon or Spraylon, to keep the drawings from smearing.

For special effects once the drawings on the film are completed, try to find music which can be tape recorded and played back to accompany the production. Also, if you can rent the movie, "Fiddle-de-dee" by Norman McLaren, your students will enjoy seeing a professional production using this technique.

ANNOTATED BIBLIOGRAPHY

Anderson, Bert. "Cameraless Animation: How It Can Turn Kids On," *Film Library Quarterly* (Winter 1972-73):27-30.
The author explains the process of drawing directly onto 16mm film. Emphasis is placed on the ease with which this may be accomplished.

"The Basics of Cinematography" (1977). Eastman Kodak Company, Department 454, Rochester, NY 14650.
A 16mm color sound film with an illustrated script that explores the basics of filmmaking. Also available on super 8mm.

Brown, James W., and Richard B. Lewis, Eds. *AV Instructional Technology Manual for Independent Study.* 5th ed. New York: McGraw-Hill Book Co., 1977, pp. 54, 63-66.
The authors show the procedure for how to draw directly onto 16mm film. A precise chapter is also available on the basics of making motion pictures and film editing. Illustrated.

Brown, James W., Richard B. Lewis, and Fred F. Harcleroad. *AV Instruction: Technology, Media, and Methods.* 5th ed. New York: McGraw-Hill, 1977, pp. 223-46.
The authors discuss the role and importance of motion pictures in the curriculum. A variety of ways to use film is set forth. Illustrated.

Cheharbakhshi, Henry, producer. *A Film about Filmmaking*; *Making a Sound Film*; *A Film about Film Editing*; and *A Film about Cinematography*. International Film Bureau, Inc., 332 South Michigan Ave., Chicago, Illinois 60604.
All of these 16mm films serve as an introduction to the individual beginning in filmmaking. Varying in length from 13 minutes to 17 minutes, they rent for $10-$12.50 each.

Filmmaking Fundamentals. 16mm, 20 minutes, color. Brown-Collen Productions, 1972. $275 sale, $20 rental.
Introduces students to basic cinematic techniques and stages involved in making super 8mm movies for a variety of instructional areas.

Fiddle-de-dee. 16mm, color, 4 minutes (Distributed by International Film Bureau, Inc., 332 South Michigan Ave., Chicago, IL 60604.) 1947. $65 sale, $6 rental.

The most widely acclaimed film by Norman McLaren in which the artist has painted directly on the film using celluloid dyes, inks, and transparent paints.

Films and Fun. 8 color sound filmstrips, 8 cassettes. AIMS Instructional Media Services, Inc., 626 Justin Avenue, Glendale, CA 91201. $160 series; $20 each part.

The series includes the basic steps in producing an 8mm film. Topics covered are an introduction to filmmaking, cameras and films, using the camera, editing, splicing up the film, animation, storyboard and titles, and sound tracking.

Hobson, Andrew, and Mark Hobson. *Film Animation as a Hobby.* New York: Sterling Publishing, 1975.

The authors explore all areas of filmmaking from basic equipment needed to special types of animation, such as collage, three-dimensional, time-lapse, cel, and pixilation. Easy to understand, step-by-step procedures. Editing the film is also shown. Illustrated.

How to Animate a Gingerbread Boy. 16mm, color, 14 min., 1973. A Rainy Day Film. Churchill Films, 662 North Robertson Blvd., Los Angeles, CA 90069. $195 sale (including book).

Nine animation techniques are explored in a story about a gingerbread boy. A 125-page illustrated booklet is included which demonstrates the techniques.

Kemp, Jerrold E. *Planning and Producing Audiovisual Materials.* 3rd ed. New York: Thomas Y. Crowell, 1975, pp. 223-64.

The author devotes an entire chapter to "Motion Pictures." Background information as well as techniques for photography, types of camera shots, and film editing are given. The rationale for using 8mm film is also discussed. Illustrated.

Matzkin, Myron A. *Super 8mm Movie Making Simplified.* Englewood Cliffs, NJ: Prentice-Hall, 1975.

The fundamentals of super 8mm moviemaking techniques and equipment are covered.

Mohr, Nelda, and Thalia-Mann Tissot. "Cents and Non-Cents of AV Crafts," *Top of the News* (January 1972):173-78.

The authors discuss and list the equipment and price for a variety of film programs from cutout animation to live action starting with zero funding up to $7.00. Cost of the hardware is not given.

Movies with a Purpose. Eastman Kodak Company, 1187 Ridge Road West, Rochester, NY 14650. Free.
A helpful brochure that explains the basics of the single-concept film and the steps involved in planning and shooting it. Illustrated.

Neighbors. 16mm, color, 9 min. National Film Board of Canada (Distributed by International Film Bureau Inc., 332 South Michigan Ave., Chicago, IL 60604.), 1952. $135 sale, $10 rental.
Norman McLaren employs pixilation to show a parable of how two friends come to blows over the possession of a flower.

101 Great Filmmaking Tips. Editors of *Super8Filmaker*, P.O. Box 10052, Department H1004, Palo Alto, CA 94303.
An information pamphlet by the editors of *Super8Filmaker* magazine. Provides numerous useful tips for the individual just beginning to explore filmmaking. Also explains how to make money to help pay for your equipment investment.

Ryan, Steve S. "Teaching Film," *Audiovisual Instruction* (September 1977):38-39.
The author discusses the importance of "film literacy" in the curriculum. Fourteen steps are discussed in ways to educate students to understand the message a film conveys.

Sights, Karen. "Animation . . . Pixilation . . . Creation for Kids," *Media Spectrum* (1976):29-30, 32.
The author discusses not only the educational implications of using film in the curriculum, but also details the steps in planning such a production. Illustrated.

Wagner, Betty Jane, and E. Arthur Stunard. *Making and Using Inexpensive Classroom Media.* Palo Alto, CA: Education Today Company, Inc., 1975, pp. 75-79.
The authors in their chapter on moviemaking briefly discuss live action and animation using super 8mm film. A section on planning and procedure for filming is included. Illustrated.

Wittich, Walter A., and Charles F. Schuller. *Instructional Technology: Its Nature and Use.* 5th ed. New York: Harper and Row, 1973, pp. 451-502.
The authors in addition to discussing the nature of film communication and research in motion picture learning also review the process involved in selecting, teaching, and learning with motion pictures. Illustrated.

Yulsman, Jerry. *The Complete Book of 8mm (Super-8, Single-8, Standard-8) Moviemaking.* New York: Coward, McCann, and Geoghegan, 1972.
The most comprehensive coverage of all aspects of 8mm filmmaking is given in simple, explicit details. Illustrated.

SUPPLIERS OF EQUIPMENT AND SOFTWARE

In order to compare prices and features on different brands of super 8mm cameras, projectors, and editing equipment, you will want to write to the following:

EPOI
Photo Products Division
101 Crossways Park West
Woodbury, N.Y. 11797
(Bolex distributor)

GAF Corporation
A-V Products Division
140 West 51st Street
New York, N.Y. 10020

Eumig
Lake Success Business Park
225 Community Drive
Great Neck, N.Y. 11020

Bell & Howell Company
Audio Visual Products Division
7100 McCormick Road
Chicago, IL 60645

Eastman Kodak Company
Motion Picture and A.V. Markets
 Division
343 State Street
Rochester, N.Y. 14650

From their brochures, select the equipment that gives you the most for your money.

ASA 40 Kodachrome or ASA 160 Ecktachrome film and splicing tape may be purchased from your local discount/photographic dealer.

For a discussion on the care of equipment and software items, you might want to write to Kodak, Consumer Markets Division, Rochester, N.Y. 14650 for a list of their service pamphlets. Titles included are "Care of Your Processed Kodak Movie Films," "Tips on Using Kodak Super 8 Movie Film," "Lubricating Your Processed Movies," and "Maintaining Your Still and Movie Camera and Projector." Prices range from $0.05 to $0.15 cents for each title.

CHAPTER 5

SINGLE-CAMERA TELEVISION PROGRAMS

Photo by Carlton Ramsey

Hargrave Military Academy
Chatham, Virginia

CHAPTER 5

SINGLE-CAMERA TELEVISION PROGRAMS

INTRODUCTION

Television as an entertainment medium has been with us for almost forty years. Students in today's classrooms have grown up with television. Thousands upon thousands of hours have been watched, replayed, and acted out by these students in their conversations and in their games. The medium has for many become as much a part of their lives as eating and sleeping. With such an affinity for the medium it is only natural that the integration of television into the classroom is so easily achieved and welcomed by all grade levels.

Most schools are already making use of instructional television (ITV) programming in the classroom. Several studies have consistently shown that when ITV is used to supplement and enhance regular, planned instruction, it can greatly expand the learning by students.

Most students already know what is meant by video-taping a program and instant replay. If their parents do not own a VTR and a camera, they still have a general idea from watching commercial television of the capabilities of such a system to record an event one minute and play it back the next. As I have had it explained to me by a fourth grade student: "Don't you understand; it works on the same principle as a tape recorder!"

Brown, Lewis, and Harcleroad in *AV Instruction: Technology, Media, and Methods* (1977) point to the many advantages of using television to stimulate learning: "Think of the skills students can learn as they plan and produce television programs: reading, writing, organizing, cooperating with others, speaking, directing, performing, assuming responsibility, drawing, lettering, photographing, editing, recording, advertising" (p. 260). All you as the teacher need—no matter how limited your own experience with the system—is a willingness to demonstrate the videotaping process, and the students will take over from there. As the above authors conclude: "you should be ready to let your students go to work in an environment that is ready-made for learning" (p. 260).

OBJECTIVE

To learn how to produce a video television program using only the basic recording equipment.

STRATEGIES

Introducing students to this medium is like introducing them to an old friend. The only problem you will encounter is keeping them away from the equipment long enough for you to finish with the demonstration.

It is perhaps best not to give too much advanced warning that the class is going to be working with television equipment. If you do, this is all that will be discussed for weeks before you bring it into the classroom. Therefore, I have found that a natural "turn on" to use with students in introducing television is to either have the equipment already set up in the classroom when they arrive or have the media specialist of the school bring it to the room as the class begins. Absolutely nothing has to be said on your part. Students will look first at the equipment and then at you until they realize what they are about to experience.

To protect the equipment, it is perhaps a good idea to show your students how each unit is attached to the other. If you have never had experience with putting such a system together, you are bound to be fearful the first time around. Ask the media specialist to demonstrate one time and then give it a try. If the media specialist is reluctant, then read through the manual and do it on your own. You will be surprised how simple it is. As I so often explain to students, there simply is no way to goof this up unless you try to jam a plug onto a fitting where it could not possibly go.

When you have interconnected the system and done some taping, let the students disconnect the system. As soon as they have finished, ask them to put it back together and begin taping. As long as you stay in the background and warn them *not* to touch the semicircular recording heads when threading the VTR or *not* to point the camera into direct sunlight, the system should be easily utilized by your captivated students.

Once the students have had this brief encounter with taping at random, it is a good idea to show them either a taped PBS program or a short half-hour commercial program and have them analyze 1) how they think the program was put together, 2) the different camera angles used, 3) the number of cameras used in the production, and 4) how many individuals were involved in making the program complete. Such an exercise helps to make them consider the time taken to produce a quality program.

Also, if you are going to take the time to explore the capabilities of television in the school setting with students, it is useful from an informational and motivational standpoint to visit a local television studio. Most stations are willing to schedule groups in for a tour and a question-and-answer session.

If these strategies are used to get students interested in using the medium, you will have no problem stopping long enough to decide on a topic to research, develop, storyboard, and script for production.

DEFINITION OF TERMS

Single-camera television: Limited to the use of only one camera to visually record the program; all shots must be arranged so that one shot will smoothly lead into the next; most single-camera units should consist of a zoom lens, viewfinder, and tripod; some cameras, such as the portapak camera, come equipped with a built-in microphone and *small* monitor for reviewing the taped program.

Zoom lens: Lens attached to the camera unit which allows you to move in close or farther away from the subject without moving the camera tripod.

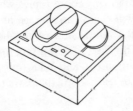

Viewfinder: Attachment that is mounted on top of the camera to check the picture image; you will want to check the subject you are taping using the viewfinder *before* you begin your actual recording.

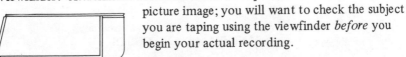

VTR: Stands for video(V) tape(T) recorder(R); the picture and the sound are recorded onto the videotape; a basic VTR will allow you to record the picture and the sound from a production and play it back for viewing on a monitor; some units allow for recording of sound *after* the picture has been recorded and some degree of editing capability to remove or insert segments after the initial taping.

Monitor/receiver: A television receiver which enables you to watch the production as you tape to be certain you are recording what you are seeing through the camera; monitors/receivers may also serve as a receiver so that you can record and replay programs on regular broadcast channels.

Videotape: Magnetic tape which has been specially designed to store both a picture and sound for playback; most VTR units for classroom use are built to take ½" videotape; depending upon the machine you purchase, videotape is either stored on an open reel of 30-60 minutes in recording length or on a 3/4" cassette of the same time.

cassette

reel to reel

Portapak unit: Portable television unit which may run on charged batteries or may be plugged into an electrical outlet; it is portable because one person can carry the pack which consists of the VTR and hold the camera which has a built-in microphone and monitor for playback viewing.

MATERIALS AND COSTS

Videotape equipment is expensive—there is simply no way to avoid that fact. If you can afford to purchase a color system, do so. Students are attracted to color since most have it in their homes. Beyond this, there are many more topics which will be enhanced by the use of color. A color system will run on an average of $3500-$5000 including the camera, monitor, and VTR. Even if color cannot be afforded, I would opt to purchase a black and white unit instead of waiting for more funding. A comparable black and white camera, monitor, and VTR unit should total about $2200. Students should be willing to learn all of the basic techniques before advancing to a more expensive system.

Quality tape from 3M, Ampex, or Memorex, if available on state contract, might run between $13 for 30 minutes to $22 for 60 minutes. If not available, you should expect to pay between $22 to $40 for the same tapes. Any one of these brands give excellent black and white or color resolution. Videocassette tapes varying in length from 30-60 minutes sell for $12-$20.

SUMMARY LIST OF ESTIMATED COSTS

Equipment

Item	Estimated Cost
color system	
VTR: reel to reel	$1350
cassette	1450
monitor (22")	800
camera	1700
black and white system	
VTR: reel to reel	900
monitor (22")	400
camera with viewfinder, zoom lens, and tripod	1000

Software

tapes			
reel to reel:	30 minutes	22
	60 minutes	40
cassette:	30 minutes	12
	60 minutes	20

PROCEDURE FOR PRODUCTION

From my point of view, the key to a successful single-camera television program is the advanced planning that goes into it before the camera and VTR are even turned on. I have witnessed too many frustrating first encounters by teachers and students alike simply because they felt that the finished product could be written, directed, and taped all in one meeting—IMPOSSIBLE.

As I mentioned in the "Strategies" section, one of the best ways to turn students on to the medium is with an initial introduction/demonstration/discussion of its capabilities. After the initial introduction to the video system, the following steps might be taken in planning and producing the finished program:

1. Decide on a simple topic and develop the storyboard. You might want to be thinking about different positions for the camera, such as close-up, medium or long shots that will add variety for the viewer and write these down under the picture as "special instructions."

2.   Convert the storyboard to a script format. You should consider at this stage of development adding an additional column not usually included in scripting—the camera column (check the "sample format" section for an example of this). The column is useful for the director of the program to check the sequence of events at a glance. Also, while scripting, it will help if you record an estimated time for each sequence under the video. More than likely this will change, but the students need to know an estimated running time before the taping begins.

3.   Choose the roles to be played by students. In addition to the actors, other very important people in the production are the camera person; the technicians who check the sound level, set up and maintain the entire VTR system; the set manager who checks for placement of all the props; and the director who controls all the rehearsals and taping sessions. Some programs will require a narrator who introduces and ties the production together periodically. Also, depending upon the number and type of visuals to be used, a graphics committee may have to be formed. If visuals are used, keep the lettering large and the pictures as simple as possible.

4.   Rehearse the program as much as possible *before* taping. Even though in working with videotape you have the capability of retaking the program until the group feels it is of acceptable quality, it is much better to work out the problem areas before the tape begins to roll.

5.   Try to arrange for an area or room for your rehearsals and final taping that is free of interruption from other classes and is away from external noise. Most microphones used with the VTR are sensitive and tend to pick up all extraneous noise. Constant interruptions by other students or from a school intercom greatly disturb the concentration of the group.

6.   If at all possible, do not *pause* the tape. Most VTR systems have a pause which will allow you to stop the tape without taking the machine out of the record mode. Unless your system is highly sophisticated, you will not be able to remove the blur that results from the pause. Therefore, keep your tape moving from start to finish.

7.   If you continue to use the VTR system in your classroom and your group is upper elementary or above, you might want to rent "The Electronic Rainbow: Television" (referenced in the bibliography) for viewing. This movie is an excellent, up-to-date overview of all aspects of video taping.

SAMPLE FORMAT

Four high school seniors planned the instructional lesson on changing a flat tire. With the aid of their teacher they developed the objective, grade level, range, pre-lesson, length, actual lesson, follow-up activity and bibliography. In the script, they have added a division for the camera with instructions for positions: close-up, medium or long shots. Approximate running time for each section is recorded under the video in parentheses. The narrator speaks the audio throughout the program even though the camera is not on him continuously.

LESSON PLAN

TITLE:	PROCEDURE FOR CHANGING A FLAT TIRE
OBJECTIVE:	To present safe and proper procedure for changing a flat tire.
GRADE LEVEL:	Senior high through adult education.
PRE-LESSON:	The instructor might wish to tell a story of how he had to change a tire and the difficulty that he experienced. Also, he might have the equipment necessary for changing a tire and review this with his audience.
LENGTH:	Five minutes.
THE LESSON:	This lesson will show certain safety precautions one should follow in the event of a flat tire. Also, the step-by-step procedure of changing the flat tire will be shown.
FOLLOW-UP:	If possible, actually change a tire.

BIBLIOGRAPHY

Lane, A. R., and Pawlowski, J. G. *Tomorrow's Drivers*. New York: Harper and Row, 1965.

Ward, Roger, and Yates, Brock. *Guide to Good Driving*. Chicago: Lyons and Carnahan, Inc., 1967.

(Script begins on page 108)

SCRIPT

Camera	Video	Audio
on title card	Procedure for Changing a Flat Tire (60 sec)	
move slowly to Bill and then to car (long shot)	narrator (Bill) and car being driven behind Bill	If a tire should blow out or go flat, keep your head. Hold the steering wheel firmly, and don't allow it to be torn from your grasp. Remove your foot from the accelerator and concentrate on steering until the speed of the car has decreased to about 10-15 mph. Then begin braking gently, get out of the stream of traffic as quickly as possible, and stop in a safe place.
	(30 sec.)	
move to Tim and close-up of equipment	demonstrator (Tim) and equipment	Here we have a typical young driver involved with the task of changing a flat tire. The equipment used for most cars are a jack, broken into 4 parts (jack stand, jack lever, jack handle, and the jack itself) and a spare tire.
follow Tim to ready the car (medium shot)	demonstrator (Tim) and car	In order to change a tire 1) Set the parking brake and move the gear selector to Park. On a standard transmission car, shift to Reverse. If possible, block front or rear wheels. 2) Raise the hood and activate the emergency flashers or place some other warning device at an ample distance to the front and rear to warn drivers.
	(20 sec.)	

SCRIPT (cont'd)

Camera	Video	Audio
follow Tim to tire and jack (close-up)	demonstrator (Tim) and tire with jack	3) With a screwdriver or the flat end of a jack handle, pry off the hubcap from the wheel. Loosen the wheel nuts slightly with the tire wrench. 4) Position the jack as the *owner's manual indicates.* Jack the wheel off the ground after making sure the jack stands straight and will not slip.
	(80 sec.)	Remove the wheel nuts and pull off wheel. 5) Put on the spare tire and replace all the nuts by hand. With the wrench, tighten the two opposite nuts firmly to position the wheel correctly, then tighten the rest of the
	(40 sec.)	nuts with your hands. (pause)
follow to jack (close-up)	demonstrator (Tim) and jack	Lower the jack and tighten all the nuts securely with the wrench. Place the hub cap back on with a sharp blow of your hand, and put away your equipment and the damaged tire. As soon as you can, get the damaged tire
	(40 sec.)	repaired.
move to Bill (medium shot)	narrator (Bill)	Conclusion: Thank you. We hope this information will help you in an emergency when you need to
	(10 sec.)	be able to change a tire.

ANNOTATED BIBLIOGRAPHY

Anderson, Chuck. *The Electric Journalist: An Introduction to Video.* New York: Praeger Publishers, 1973.
Covers the basic principles of videotape recording and methods of utilization. The author also includes a handy list of "things to do with the videotape machine."

Brown, James W., and Richard B. Lewis, Eds. *AV Instructional Technology Manual for Independent Study.* 5th ed. New York: McGraw-Hill, 1977, pp. 67-70.
A step-by-step approach is taken in the single-camera television production unit detailed by these authors. Production strategy, lighting, audio, mechanics of editing, graphic materials and advantages of portable video equipment are all discussed. Illustrated.

Brown, James W., Richard B. Lewis, and Fred F. Harcleroad. *AV Instruction: Technology, Media, and Methods.* 5th ed. New York: McGraw-Hill, 1977, pp. 248-68.
The authors discuss the many uses of television in and out of the school setting. In addition to reviewing methods of utilization of ITV in the classroom, they also show how portable video tape equipment may be used to produce simple television programs. Illustrated.

The Electronic Rainbow: Television. 16mm, color, 23 min. Pyramid Films, Box 1048, Santa Monica, CA 90406, 1977. $325 sale, $35 rental.
Leonard Nimoy surveys the development of television and then discusses basic principles and mechanisms of broadcasting along with a brief overview of different kinds of TV systems.

"Getting It on Video." Media Works, Department 1, Route 2, Box 798, Tucson, AZ 85715, 1977. Videocassettes, Series 1, $295; Series 2, $295 or Sound-filmstrips, Series 1, $125; Series 2, $125.
Both series contain six, in-depth topics discussing the ins and outs of working with a video system. Individual sound-filmstrip titles may be purchased for $30 each.

Harwood, D. *Everything You Always Wanted to Know about Video Tape Recording.* 2nd ed. Queens, NY: VTR Publishing Co., 1975.
The author has designed the book in a question/answer format. An analysis of the history, equipment, production, and maintenance of video tape recording is included along with an extensive list of defined terms. Illustrated.

Kahn, Linda. "VTR in the Classroom—or—How I Learned to Stop Worrying and Start Saving Cardboard Boxes," *Media & Methods* (April 1975):40-41.

An English teacher of seventh and ninth grade students explains how she teaches media-oriented courses with the aid of the VTR system.

Kemp, Jerrold E. *Planning and Producing Audiovisual Materials.* 3rd ed. New York: Thomas Y. Crowell, 1975, pp. 265-74.
The author discusses special requirements of television and how to prepare materials for display. A variety of materials are covered: easels, felt boards, hook-and-loop boards, magnetic boards, and the use of photographs, slides, filmstrips, transparencies, and motion pictures with television. Illustrated.

Ray, Mary L. "Videotaping: You and Your Kids Can Do It," *Teacher* (January 1975):47-48, 106.
The author covers the use of videotaping as an integral part of the classroom. Suggestions are given on how to proceed with making your own production. Illustrated.

Robinson, Richard. *The Video Primer.* New York: Links Book Publishers, 1974.
A guide to equipment, software, and production techniques.

Robson, Walt. "Getting Your Bait Back," *Video Systems* (March 1977):44-46.
The author takes a step-by-step approach to writing the videotape script without the professional script writer. Especially helpful is the information on storyboarding. Illustrated.

Rosenberg, Kenyon C., and John S. Doskey. *Media Equipment: A Guide and Dictionary.* Littleton, CO: Libraries Unlimited, 1976.
The guide section gives criteria for evaluating and selecting AV equipment, and the dictionary section defines 400 media terms.

Taylor, Charles B. "To Videotape or Not to Videotape," *Audiovisual Instruction* (January 1977): 33-34, 39-40.
The author explains how he promotes his students' exploration of Shakespeare using videotape. The reasons for using videotape over the traditional term paper and the steps to put the production together are discussed.

Tucker, Nancy J. "What You Always Wanted to Know about VTR: Once Over Lightly," *Media Spectrum* (1974):14-15, 23.
The author attempts to put the reader at ease by explaining why the VTR system is not as fragile as most think it is. Three basic units are briefly covered: videorecorder and a camera kit with viewfinder, a portapak, and a videocassette recorder and a camera kit.

Winslow, Ken, ed. *Video Play Program Source Guide.* Ridgefield, CT: C. S. Tepfer Publishing Co., 1974.
Lists around 140 companies which handle video software and gives their prices.

Wittich, Walter A., and Charles F. Schuller. *Instructional Technology: Its Nature and Use.* 5th ed. New York: Harper and Row, 1973, pp. 503-550.
The authors devote an entire chapter specifically to the utilization of instructional television in the classroom. Research findings as well as ways to incorporate ITV in the curriculum are detailed. Illustrated.

SUGGESTIONS FOR FOLLOW-UP ACTIVITIES

Once your students have gained experience and a certain degree of confidence in their abilities to write, produce, and direct a single-camera program, they may want to tackle one or all of the suggested follow-up activities listed below:

1.　Students of all age levels enjoy acting out either ad-lib situations or events of an historical or contemporary nature. I have witnessed some excellent presentations such as this where teachers have written down events in history that the students have been studying and asked them to act out the situations as they understood them. When recorded on videotape, students participating in the presentation have the opportunity to replay and evaluate their production. If a mistake has been made, additional research into the topic and another taping might help to clear up the problem areas.

2.　Using videotaping for making a visual term paper is one option for students who feel restricted by the traditional written method. The same amount of time, sometimes more, is required of the student to put together a program that is both informationally and visually accurate and appealing.

3.　If a portapak unit is available, students might want to research a local topic and do taping on location. Also, if a field trip is taken by the group, this is an excellent time to take a portapak along and record different segments for discussion when the group returns to the classroom.

4.　If you can borrow another single-camera unit from another school or district, your students should enjoy demonstrating the step-by-step procedure of putting the VTR system together so that other students—and teachers— could replay the tape and learn individually.

5.　Current events of the school, such as athletic games, plays, and special speakers may be taped for future viewing by students already familiar with the technique.

6.　Special experiments in chemistry, biology, or other science classes that might be too costly to repeat might be taped and played back in the media center for individual review.

7.   Once the other nonprint areas discussed in this handbook have been tried and refined, your students might want to record on tape the procedures to share with other students, schools, or the district.

SUPPLIERS OF EQUIPMENT AND SOFTWARE

Since both the equipment and the software are expensive items, you will want to investigate the costs extensively before buying. So that you have adequate background on what different brands of cameras, video tape recorders, and monitors have to offer, write to three of the leaders in the field:

Sony Corporation of America
VTR Division
9 West 57th Street
New York, N.Y. 10019

JVC Industries, Inc.
58-75 Queens Midtown Expressway
Maspeth, N.Y. 11378

Panasonic Company
Video Systems Division
1 Panasonic Way
Secaucus, N.J., 07094

If you request in your letter, they will send you the names of local dealers. These dealers should be willing to demonstrate their equipment. It will be up to you to write the specifications. Some suggestions on writing bid specifications and definition of terms is given in Kenyon C. Rosenberg and John S. Doskey's *Media Equipment: A Guide and Dictionary* (1976). Once you have done this, be sure to send these specifications out for open bids. This will help you get more for your money.

Tapes for the VTR should be purchased from your local dealers or if a state contract is available, then this will probably be the cheapest way to buy. You might also want to write to these three companies for comparative pricing:

3M Company
Video Products Division
3M Center
St. Paul, Minnesota 55101

Memorex Corporation
San Thomas at Central Expressway
Santa Clara, California 95052

Ampex Corporation
401 Broadway
Redwood City, California 94063

CHAPTER 6

TRANSPARENCY LIFTS AND STORY LAMINATION

White Rock Elementary School
Richardson, Texas

CHAPTER 6

TRANSPARENCY LIFTS AND
STORY LAMINATION

INTRODUCTION

Making transparency lifts and laminating flat pictures are two techniques that I have found are *always* successful in turning kids on to print (from elementary through senior high school) using nonprint. There is a real inward satisfaction gained by the student when he is successful with lifting a clay base picture onto a piece of clear plastic film, or when he laminates a series of his own drawings or even pictures from a magazine to form a story for others to see and/or use. The common responses that I have had when going through this activity with kids are "I never dreamed I could do that," "It was so easy," "Let's do it again," and "I've got to take it home to show Mom and Dad so I can hang it in my room." Once you have tried either or both of these activities, I am sure you will agree with the above.

There are numerous other activities which could be covered which are related to transparency lifts and story lamination (some of these are briefly discussed in the "Suggestions for Follow-Up Activities"). However, from past experience, you should try these activities first and if the enthusiasm continues, you might want to attempt the follow-up activities.

OBJECTIVES

To learn how to lift color clay base pictures in order to make overhead transparencies.

To be able to laminate flat pictures for use in relating stories or a sequence of events.

STRATEGIES

Some of the students you will choose to take part in these activities will never have seen a transparency or a laminated picture. Therefore, showing them each item is important so they will have a frame of reference from the beginning. If you have a clear acetate sheet and transparency marking pens or if you have any type of clear plastic, such as plastic sandwich bags and some translucent paints, you can mark or paint on the plastic, hold it up to the light and show the students how they can see right through it. After this, place your markings onto the overhead projector and display your creation on a screen or the wall.

When you have shown them how translucent configurations can be projected, take a clay base picture from a magazine (to test for clay base, place a dab of water on one corner of the picture and rub; if the picture does not dissolve and if when gently rubbing the corner a white chalky residue comes up, then more than likely you have a clay base picture). Hold it up to the light—students will not be able to see through it. Then place it onto the overhead projector—again, students will only see a black blob on the screen. Ask them why the picture cannot be projected— the answer should be obvious: the picture is not translucent; thus, light will not shine through it!

If your students at this stage appear inquisitive and want to know if projection of this picture is ever possible—the most students will want to know at this stage—then explain that this is possible, but the process is really messy. If you did not have them before, you will now. There is nothing better to get students excited than making a creative mess in the classroom or media center.

With making story laminations I use another approach to involve the students. In my files I always keep drawings and cutouts from magazines that have not been laminated, but that have been used either in class for lecture-discussion periods or for bulletin boards. Usually I do not even have to comment on the condition of either—students recognize at first glance that the edges of the pictures are frayed, some have been torn, and indeed some should never be used again considering their wrinkled condition. Is there a remedy for future use of pictures and/or student drawings that I wish to keep on file for presentation? Yes. If you have a driver's license, your picture was probably protected by laminating film and this can be shown to the students. If you do not have such a picture on hand, almost all drug-discount stores have a machine that can laminate a picture which you can show to the class.

DEFINITION OF TERMS

Transparency lift: A method used to transfer a clay base picture onto clear plastic film so that the picture becomes translucent and can be projected on an overhead projector; the original picture is actually sealed onto the laminating film with heat and the clay base backing is washed away (see photograph on top of page 119).

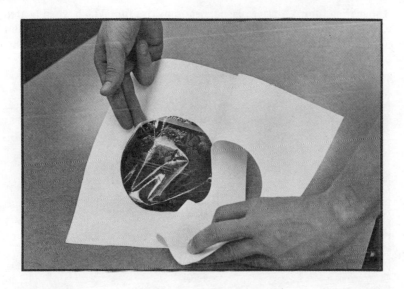

Lamination: A process whereby a picture or drawing is protected using a clear plastic film placed over the top of the original.

© General Foods Corporation 1977, reprinted with permission of General Foods Corporation

Laminating film: A clear plastic, heat-sensitive film which when heated to a certain temperature will adhere to another surface; this particular kind of film may be used for transparency lifts or for lamination.

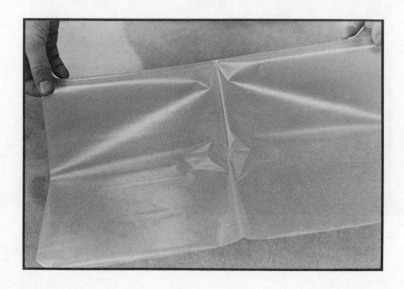

Dry mount press: A machine made especially for the dry mount and lamination process; the upper plate temperature may be regulated according to the process so that heat is evenly distributed over the item.

Dry mount tissue: A specially treated paper (see top of page 121) which when heated to a prescribed temperature melts the glue on both sides so that a picture or drawing will adhere to another surface such as posterboard or construction paper.

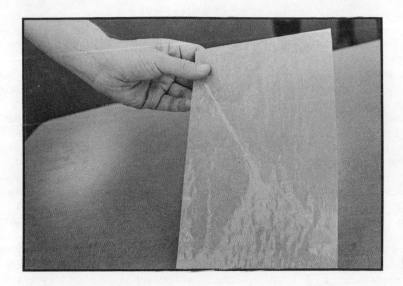

Tacking iron: A heating iron used to tack the dry mount tissue and the laminating film to the object before placement into the dry mount press; by using the tacking iron, you insure that the tissue and film will not move.

Mounting frame: A precut cardboard frame with a display opening so that the transparency may be taped onto it for ease in handling and storage.

MATERIALS AND COSTS

The most expensive item to be purchased in the equipment line is the dry mount press. A variety of sizes are available; however, you need to determine which machine will meet your continued needs for dry mounting and laminating. The best advice is to buy the largest press that your budget will allow. If you are forced into choosing and your budget is limited, then strike a compromise and purchase the 12x15-inch medium size press for around $175. Other items in the equipment line include a tacking iron for $20.00, a good pair of cutting shears for around $2.00, and a couple of X-ACTO® knives with extra blades for $1.50 each.

Software for these processes is not inexpensive, but if bought in sufficient quantity, money may be saved. Laminating film may be purchased by the roll; for example, a 11 1/8" by 100' roll sells for $10.00. A variety of other sizes are available. Dry mount tissue may be bought by 100 sheets boxes or the roll: $4.00-$20.00. If care is taken to keep scraps from unused pieces of both in separate boxes, students, if encouraged, will go to the scrap boxes first to see if a piece of leftover tissue or film is all that they really need to complete the project. Posterboard is something that can be bought in a variety of widths and lengths and then cut to desired specification. A single sheet of 28" x 44" posterboard will sell for $1.20-$1.50. If you want a cheaper posterboard which can be purchased in drug-discount stores, a 24" x 30" sheet would sell for $0.30 each. Construction paper, masking tape, butcher paper (or newsprint), and mounting frames are other items listed on the summary sheet which should also be purchased.

SUMMARY LIST OF ESTIMATED COSTS

Equipment

Item	Estimated Cost
dry mount press	
8½" x 11½" (small)	$100.00
12" x 15" (medium)	175.00
18½" x 15½" (large)	220.00
tacking iron	20.00
scissors	2.00
X-ACTO® knife with blades	1.50

Software

laminating film	
roll (11 1/8" x 100')	$ 10.00
dry mount tissue	
box of 100 sheets (8½" x 11")	4.00
roll (24" x 50 yds.)	20.00
poster board (28" x 44")	1.30
construction paper (50 sheets)	1.00

SUMMARY LIST OF ESTIMATED COSTS (cont'd)

Item	Estimated Cost
masking tape (1 roll)	$ 0.75
mounting frames (1 box of 100)	14.00
butcher paper ($0.02 per foot—200')	2.00
cotton balls (1 large package)	1.25

PROCEDURE FOR PRODUCTION

It is very easy to begin making color lifts and laminating pictures without any particular goal beyond simply mastering the two processes—this appears at first glance to be worthy in and of itself, and indeed it is; however, much, too much laminating film can be and is wasted by over-learning both processes. It is much better to demonstrate the technique using the step-by-step procedures discussed here and then begin working from the storyboard so that the activity will be completed within your pre-established time boundaries.

It is also very easy to have both lifting and laminating going on at the same time since the same machine is used; however, be sure that you divide the room in half so that half the group is on one side and half on the other. You will be using water for lifting, and watermarks on pictures to be laminated are not attractive.

Checklist for Setting Up the Demonstration

1. Dry mounting a picture onto posterboard
   a. Set the dry mount press on 225°

2.   Find a clay base picture or article from a newspaper.

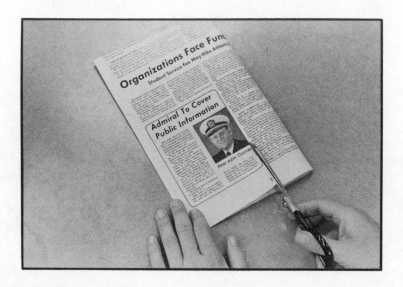

Courtesy of The North Texas Daily

3.   Tack a piece of dry mount tissue to the center of the picture or article with the tacking iron.

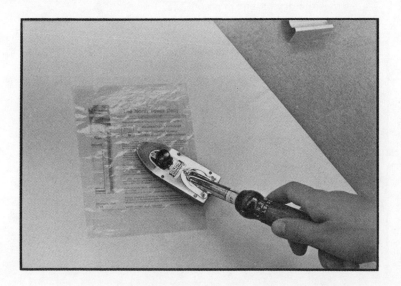

4.   Trim the tissue and picture/article so that *no* tissue may be seen beyond the edges.

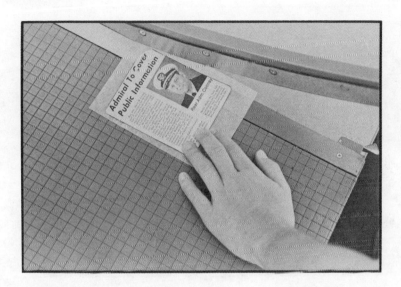

5.   Place the picture/article on the posterboard and holding the center in place with the fingers, lift up each side and tack the corners to the posterboard.

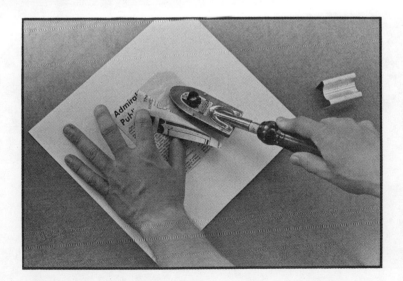

6.   Slip the completed work between the butcher paper (or newsprint) to protect the posterboard and the press.

7.   Place the sandwich in the pre-heated 225° dry mount press for about 45-60 seconds.

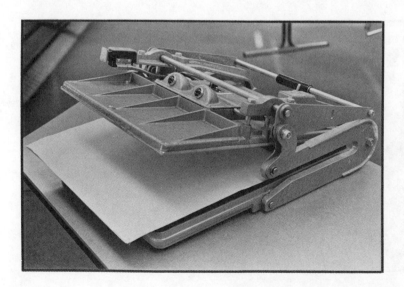

8.   Remove. Check the edges for a complete seal between the picture/ article and the posterboard. If incomplete, place back into the press for another 45 seconds.

In humid areas, it is always a good idea to dry the pictures or articles before you begin to work; this removes all the moisture content. Simply place the item you wish to laminate and/or lift in the butcher paper in a preheated press of 180° for around 2 minutes, remove and let cool. This simple step will greatly improve the quality of your work.

Laminating the Dry Mounted Picture/Article

1.   Set the press on 300° and allow time to heat up.

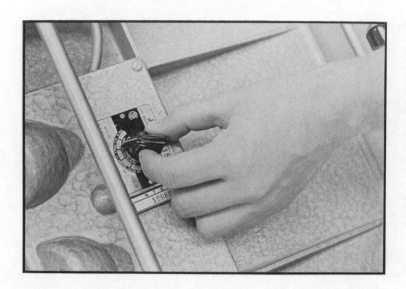

2.   Using a piece of laminating film, cover the entire posterboard. Make sure the dull side is against the posterboard.

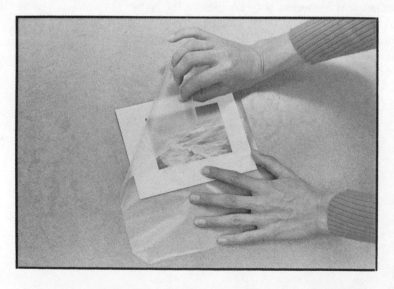

Courtesy of Coronet Films (photo above and on pp. 129-30)

3.   Tack the edges of the film with the tacking iron to the posterboard to hold it secure.

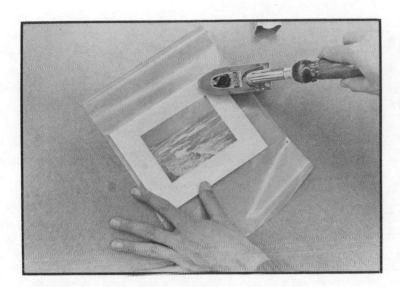

4.   Insert this between another piece of clean butcher paper for protection and place in the press for around 2 minutes.

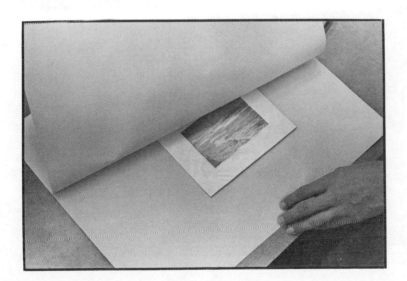

5. Remove and place under a weight *or* under a number of books so that while cooling, the posterboard will remain flat.

6. Once cooled, trim away all edges of excess film.

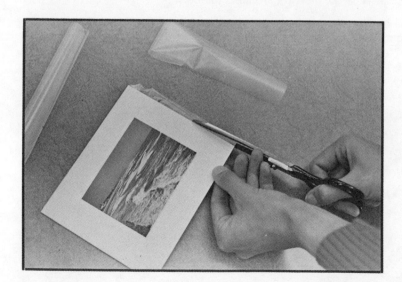

If you have a dry mount press which has been used for a number of years or even one that has not, you may want to increase the amount of pressure on the item you are laminating by lifting the bottom pad up and putting a Masonite board or folded newspaper underneath. This will increase the pressure and should improve the seal between the film and the posterboard.

Color Lifting for Transparencies

1.   Set the dry mount press for 300°.

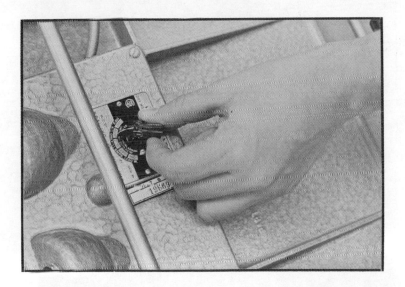

2.   Select a clay base picture from a magazine such as *National Geographic*, *People*, *Us*, *et cetera*. Test the picture on the side *not* to be lifted by rubbing a small amount of water on one corner. If a chalky residue comes up and the picture does not dissolve, it is clay base. (See photograph on page 132.)

Reprinted by special permission of LEARNING, The Magazine for Creative Teaching, December 1977 (photographs this page and 133-36).

3.   Trim the picture to the desired size and cover with laminating film. Leave excess film beyond the picture for placement in the transparency mounting frame.

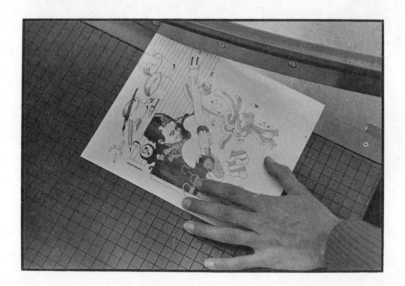

4.   Tack the corners of the film with a picture underneath to the butcher paper to hold it secure. Remember to have the dull side of the film *against* the picture you wish to lift.

5.   Sandwich this between a top and bottom layer of butcher paper and insert into the dry mount press for 2 minutes.

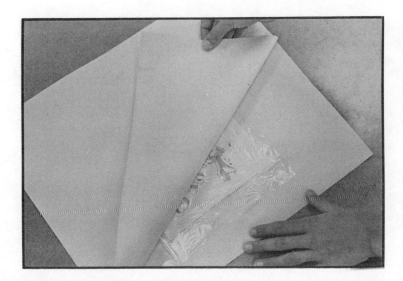

6.   Remove from the press and the sandwich, and place the laminated picture into soapy water (the same that you would normally wash dishes in). Allow to stand for around 5 minutes.

7.   Take out of the water and gently peel away the butcher paper *and the picture.*

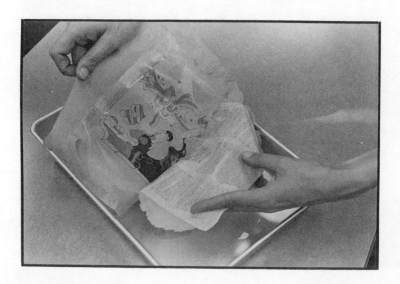

8.   Remove the clay residue using clean cotton balls. Rub in a circular motion until completely cleaned. Let dry by hanging with a clothespin.

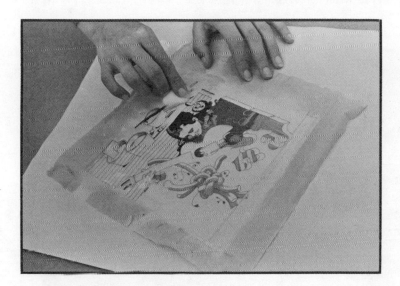

9.   When the lift is thoroughly dry, tape the shiny side down to a piece of cardboard. Using either a clear acrylic spray *or* a clear floor wax, spread an even, thin coat over the lift with a clean brush and let dry.

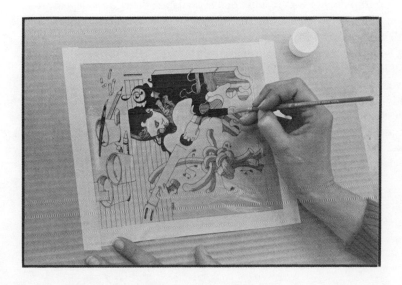

10. Remove from the cardboard and tape the lift onto a mounting frame. If the picture you have lifted is too small for a regular size mount, use posterboard and an X-ACTO® knife and cut out a frame that is the right size.

After reading through all of the above, you should have noticed that the dry mount press has to be set on different temperatures. If you have *two* presses, you will have no trouble; however, if only one is available, then you will want to complete as much of the dry mounting first *before* laminating and lifting begins. The press will not heat and cool as rapidly as you might like. Also, be careful when working with the press and the tacking irons to warn the students not to play around this equipment. I have never experienced any bad burns since I have always warned everyone in advance of what could possibly happen.

It is important to note that this procedure is messy. The mess can easily get out of control if your students are not advised in advance to clean up as much as possible as they progress through the steps. If the areas are kept clean, there is less likelihood that a most unusual color lift or a well-laminated picture will be ruined by particles of dust or water spots.

SAMPLE FORMAT

The following presentation was written and planned by a seventh grade world history class studying multi-cultural people and their customs. Both formats were used by the class—color transparency lifts and story lamination. An interesting comparison and contrast of the strengths and weaknesses of both were attached after the project was completed.

TITLE: STUDENTS OF THE WORLD

PLANNING: Seventh grade students had been studying different
                    cultures and their particular customs for four weeks prior
                    to the beginning of the project. Using pictures from
                    discarded *National Geographics, Life, Time*, and any
                    other clay-based magazines, students first read the article
                    regarding the particular culture and then paraphrased it
                    in their own words. The pictures were then cut from the
                    magazines using single-edged razor blades.

                    One week was set aside for an explanation and practice
                    of making color transparency lifts and story lamination.
                    Half of the students decided to use one method for
                    their reports and the other half wanted to make their
                    reports in the form of a story for a bulletin board
                    display.

PROJECTS: No. 1 Color Transparency Lifts
                    Students worked first in one large group and decided on
                    which student would be responsible for which country.
                    A limitation had to be made on the countries to be dis-
                    cussed since only clay-based pictures could be used. Two
                    individuals were responsible for storyboarding the project
                    after the group discussion. After the second group meet-
                    ing in which the storyboard was presented and finalized,
                    each student worked up his or her script, decided on the
                    picture or pictures to be lifted and presented the idea to
                    the entire group. Once the program had been approved,
                    students lifted their pictures and made the transparencies.
                    The entire group placed their narration on a cassette tape
                    with a "ping" recorded to indicate the change from one
                    transparency to another. One student from the group
                    presented the project to the entire class. (Time to com-
                    plete the activity: two weeks.)

SAMPLE FORMAT (cont'd)

PROJECTS (cont'd):   No. 2 Story Lamination
Students in this group decided to laminate pictures
gathered from *one* country. All students met in a large
group and decided on the one country that they felt
needed further investigation. Two countries were picked
and then an examination of pictures available was made.
During the second meeting the students decided on
"Students of Germany" to display, storyboarded their
presentation as a group, and outlined their narration.
Two students were appointed to refine the narration.
Each student laminated his own pictures onto the same
color and same size posterboard. One student recorded
the narration onto cassette tape with a number in
sequence preceding each picture description. The
laminated story was pinned to the bulletin board with a
lettered number placed to the lower right of each picture. The cassette recording was placed next to the display
so that the other students could listen as a group or
individually. (Time to complete the activity: two weeks.)

	Strengths	Weaknesses
COLOR LIFTS:	1. Easy to store for future use.	1. Only clay-base pictures may be lifted.
	2. Easy to transport to other classrooms for presentation.	2. Some pictures were wasted since students did not get a perfect seal with the film.
STORY LAMINATION:	1. Easy to store and are not easily damaged.	1. Difficult to move to other classrooms.
	2. A variety of pictures could be laminated—no restriction to clay base.	2. Took up too much space; some pictures had to be taped to the wall.

—Barbara Harris

ANNOTATED BIBLIOGRAPHY

Brown, James W., and Richard B. Lewis, Eds. *AV Instructional Technology Manual for Independent Study.* 5th ed. New York: McGraw-Hill, 1977, pp. 31-34, 37-44.
The authors cover mounting pictures, laminating, picture lifts, and handmade, diazo, and heat-process transparencies. Illustrated.

Brown, James W., Richard B. Lewis, and Fred F. Harcleroad. *AV Instruction: Technology, Media, and Methods.* 5th ed. New York: McGraw-Hill, 1977, pp. 127-48, 180-87.
The authors present how to use, mount, and store flat pictures. An entire chapter is devoted to a discussion of "transparencies for overhead projection." Illustrated.

Brown, Robert M. *Educational Media: A Competency Approach.* Columbus, OH: Charles E. Merrill, 1973, pp. 107-141, 253-92.
In two separate self-instructional modules, the author in addition to a variety of other production processes, covers laminating and color lifting for making transparencies.

Kemp, Jerrold E. *Planning and Producing Audiovisual Materials.* 3rd ed. New York: Thomas Y. Crowell, 1975, pp. 196-222.
The author presents explicit details into the step-by-step procedure for making all types of transparencies from the necessary skills required to completion. Illustrated.

Media Production Series. Media Systems, Inc., 3637 East 7800 South, Salt Lake City, UT 84121.
In their *Media Production Series*, the following might be of interest: Heating, Laminating, Dry Mounting with Heat Press, and "Color Lift" Transparencies. Either slides or filmstrips may be purchased. Thirty-day preview allowed.

Minor, Ed, and Harvey R. Frye. *Techniques for Producing Visual Instructional Media.* New York: McGraw-Hill, 1970, pp. 59-96, 163-223.
The authors discuss mounting and laminating techniques in one chapter and producing transparencies for projection and display in another chapter. This is probably the most detailed step-by-step procedure given in any production manual. Illustrated.

Wagner, Betty J., and E. Arthur Stunard. *Making and Using Inexpensive Classroom Media.* Palo Alto, CA: Education Today Co., 1976, pp. 51-63, 81-87.
Authors devote an entire chapter to methods of "preserving" pictures. In addition to rubber cement mounting, they also describe hot press mounting and laminating materials. In another chapter the authors discuss a variety of techniques for making transparencies. Illustrated.

Wittich, Walter S., and Charles F. Schuller. *Instructional Technology: Its Nature and Use.* 5th ed. New York: Harper and Row, 1973, pp. 408-411; 95-110. A discussion of the uses of transparencies and the equipment necessary for overhead projection is given. The authors also present information on the advantages and disadvantages of using flat pictures in the curriculum. Illustrated.

SUGGESTIONS FOR FOLLOW-UP ACTIVITIES

There are so many activities directly related to making transparency lifts and story lamination, it is difficult to know where to begin and when to stop. The following are only a few ideas; you will want to experiment on your own as you and your students gain confidence:

1.   Now that you have lifted clay base pictures for overhead transparencies, you should be willing to try making slides using the same process. Students will have to be reminded that their choice of pictures will be restricted to a 1" x 1½" format for placement in cardboard or plastic slide ready mounts. The mounts may be purchased in quantities of 100 for around $4.50. Because the lamination film is flimsy, it will have to be taped and stretched onto the slide mounts, coated on the back with the clear acrylic wax, allowed to dry and then sealed into the slide mount. An entire slide-tape presentation using the same procedure in chapter 3 may be developed.

2.   Another activity which students enjoy is drawing with transparency marking pens or paints directly onto the film. It is best to mount the film in the frames first to hold it steady and to cut down on the possibility of smearing the finished work. If students wish to trace maps or outlines of drawings onto the film, the film in the mount can be placed directly over the picture. If you use a permanent ink or translucent paint you will not have to worry about the drawing smearing; however, if you use an ink that comes up when you touch it, then you will need to spray the finished product with a clear acrylic spray which can be purchased from local arts and crafts dealers. You may want to paint the back with clear floor wax to make the transparency completely translucent.

3.   A variety of items may be laminated if properly dried and flattened. Your students may wish to collect fall leaves or spring flowers and dry and press them first in the dry mount press—make sure you use the butcher paper around the items to protect the press. If you set the press on 180°, you may leave the collected item in for a few minutes to begin the drying process— don't leave them in too long or the odor will be too strong for you or your class to endure. Take them out and press between old book pages—again, use butcher paper to keep the items from sticking to the pages. After a few

days, dry and press them again in the press to remove all moisture. Students can then laminate these for display on the bulletin board.

4.   I have used the lamination process repeatedly for protecting instructional units which I knew the students would be using over and over again. By placing a protective plastic cover over the top and bottom of the worksheet, students' messy fingers or recorded answers on the sheet using a temporary felt tip ink pen or even a crayon may be wiped clean and reused. Teachers who have purchased expensive games or have taken the time to make their own have found that laminating these *before* they are used increases their circulation. With young and older students alike I have encouraged them to make their own puzzles and games. Once a picture has been dry mounted to a cardboard or posterboard backing and laminated on both sides, it may be cut into a variety of shapes for puzzle pieces.

5.   An item which you might like to write for once your students have made their own transparencies is *Polarmotion Overhead Transparencies*, free from American Polarizers, Inc., 1500 Spring Garden Street, P.O. Box 7929, Philadelphia, Pennsylvania 19101. Although it would be difficult to make these in-house, your students might like to see what can be done with still transparencies to give them animated motion. You are likely to see more and more of these on the instructional market in future years as people discover their effectiveness for certain topics.

SUPPLIERS OF EQUIPMENT AND SOFTWARE

The majority of the software items may be purchased in your local discount stores. For laminating film, dry mount tissue, dry mount press, tacking irons, and mounting frames, you might want to write to one or all of the companies listed below for comparative pricing:

Laminex Inc.
P.O. Box 577
Matthews, NC 28105

The Highsmith Co., Inc.
P.O. Box 25, Highway 106 East
Fort Atkinson, WI 53538

Seal Incorporated
550 Spring Street
Naugatuck, CN 06770

Bro-Dart
1609 Memorial Avenue
Williamsport, PA 17701

Franklin Distributors Corp.
P.O. Box 320
Denville, NJ 07834

Josten's
Library Services Division
1301 Cliff Road
Burnsville, MN 55337

CHAPTER 7

DIORAMAS

White Rock Elementary School
Richardson, Texas

CHAPTER 7

DIORAMAS

INTRODUCTION

Wittich and Schuller in *Instructional Technology: Its Nature and Use* (1973) state that "making a diorama provides an excellent means of eliciting the pupil's creative involvement in the learning experience" (p. 169). Students of all ages have used and continue to use this three-dimensional technique as a means of self-expression and personal interpretation of something viewed in real life and of something fantasized from reading or listening to a book.

Dioramas can be as elaborate or as simple as you or the students wish them to be. I have seen very expensive, realistic miniature animals, people, mountains, *et cetera*, included in dioramas which added greatly to their effectiveness, yet I have also helped students make their own miniatures for a fraction of the cost to create an equally realistic diorama. Simplicity goes a long way in producing a diorama that is pleasing to the eye of the beholder and also to the student making one for the first time.

OBJECTIVES

To learn how to make dioramas using inexpensive materials.
To become aware of the variety of dioramas that can be made.

STRATEGIES

Most students have at one time or the other viewed a type of diorama probably without even knowing that that was what it was called, such as museum displays of

145

stuffed animals in their natural habitat or even store windows during the holiday seasons. To spark their interest, you might want to take a field trip to a museum in your locale or wait until Thanksgiving or Christmas when the windows of your local stores are decorated with colorful dioramas. If you alert the students to observe how such dioramas are put together, they should be ready to produce their own once you return.

Another technique that I have used is to make miniature animals and people with popsicle sticks, felt pieces, soap carvings, scraps of yarn, and construction paper and then display the results. Once completed, I guide the students into a discussion of where they think these people and/or animals would live. This approach naturally leads into a discussion of dioramas and the procedure for making them.

When I taught English on the secondary level, I usually required some type of final project in addition to the standard writing assignments, of visualizing a story, a play, a poem or a scene from a novel we had read together. I encouraged the students to make dioramas small enough so they could either be displayed in the school media center or in a locked display case. With the diorama they had to include a typed copy of the selection they had chosen to visualize.

DEFINITION OF TERMS

Diorama: A three-dimensional scene which depicts an idea; a wide variety of materials may be used to construct the scene from cardboard to wood to plastic to paper; dioramas may vary also by type—traditional, box, cutout, open, flat-figure, or peep show. Examples of the various types of dioramas are shown below.

Traditional: A wooden frame with an attached semicircular base and background with a definite three-dimensional perspective.

Box: A scene constructed within the framework of an actual box.

Cutout: Pieces of paper pasted together to form a three-dimensional scene.

Open: Cardboard folded to form a background and ground area where the three-dimensional scene may be made.

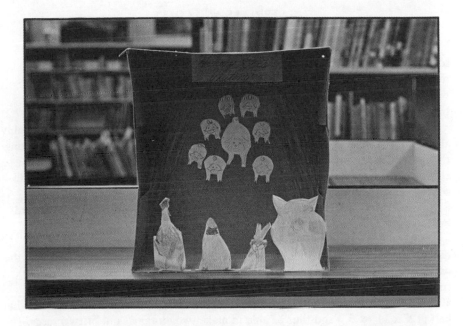

Flat-figure: Use of cut-outs attached or with tab bottoms so that they will stand upright.

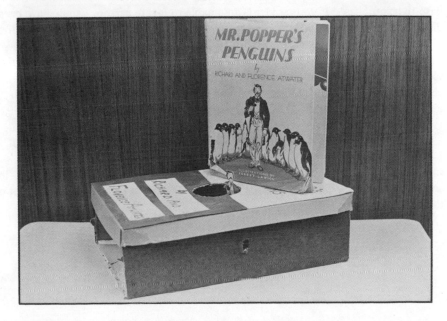

Peep show: A scene constructed within a box with an opening at the top for light and a hole at one end for viewing.

MATERIALS AND COSTS

If you are a collector of scraps of materials, inexpensive jewelry or other so-called "junk" items, you should experience little difficulty in supplying the majority of items needed to make dioramas. However, some equipment and software items will probably have to be purchased if you choose to construct the traditional diorama.

The majority of the equipment needed to construct the diorama you probably already own; if not, your students will have them at home. If you plan on repeating this activity in the future, you should purchase the necessary equipment for your classroom. A simple hand saw is all you need to cut the one-inch strips and should cost around $5.00. A hammer for nailing the frame together should run about $3.00. And an X-ACTO® knife with extra blades for cutting the heavy duty cardboard can be purchased for $1.50.

Wood strips of 1" x 1" may be purchased in varying lengths; therefore, determine first the size of the rectangular frames you wish to construct and buy the one length that will waste the least amount of wood. For example, if you decide to make the diorama 24" (top) x 22" (bottom) x 12" (sides) then you will need at least a 70" length or 2 yards for each diorama. You may wish to decrease this by half (12" x 11" x 6") and thus be able to make two dioramas out of two yards. The price of wood fluctuates greatly; currently, for 2 yards of 1" x 1" pine you should expect to pay around $1.50.

Heavy duty cardboard for the base of the diorama is another item that may have to be purchased if your students are unable to locate cartons which have been discarded from supermarkets or appliance stores. At times, cardboard can be almost as expensive as wood. Check with your local art supplier. Make sure you purchase the heavy duty cardboard and not flimsy posterboard since the entire weight of the scene will be placed on this base. Using an 18" x 24" piece of cardboard if you choose to make the large diorama, you will only be able to cut one base; however, if you make the smaller diorama, you can easily cut four bases out of the same piece. Presently, a piece of heavy duty cardboard (18" x 24") sells for $1.50.

Mat board for the traditional diorama background would have to be at least 12" high and 40" long. One sheet of mat board costs around $1.90. Other consumable items such as masking tape ($0.75 for a roll), finishing nails ($0.50 for 1 lb.), and a box of tacks ($0.50) may all be purchased or students might have a number of these items at home.

SUMMARY LIST OF ESTIMATED COSTS

Equipment

Item	Estimated Cost
saw	$5.00
hammer	3.00
X-ACTO® knife with blades	1.50
ruler	.20
scissors	2.00

Software

wood strip (2 yards)	$1.50
heavy duty cardboard (18" x 24")	1.50
mat board (32" x 40")	2.00
masking tape (1 roll)	.75
finishing nails (1 lb.)	.50
tacks (1 box)	.50
paints:	
water colors (8 color set)	2.00
tempra (3/4-oz. bottle)	.40
construction paper (50 sheets)	1.00

PROCEDURE FOR PRODUCTION

Even if your students decide to develop a story that you have shared, you will want to storyboard it using their ideas for pictures and narration so that the story will be their own and not a copy of the original. Also, if the students decide to research a topic, such as the history of the horse or different Indian tribes, you will need to develop a storyboard of their ideas. Let them fill in the "video" and "audio" on the cards as the research is completed, and lay out the cards in sequence to see if the materials are consistent in content *before* constructing the dioramas.

The following steps may be used to construct the "traditional" diorama:

1.   Decide on the desired frame measurements and mark off the sections for the four sides using a ruler and pencil (see photograph on page 152). Make a straight mark across the 1" x 1" strip where you will be cutting. Steady the wood strip on a table or bench and cut through the strip at each mark. Have a student hold the extended end of the wood to keep it from splitting (see photograph on page 152).

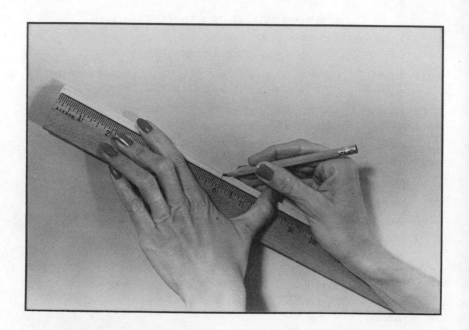

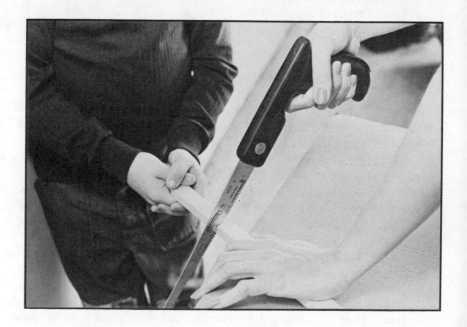

2.   Using the finishing nails, tack the frame pieces together, nailing the side pieces to the bottom first and then tacking the top on last. By placing two nails at each joint this should keep the frame from moving.

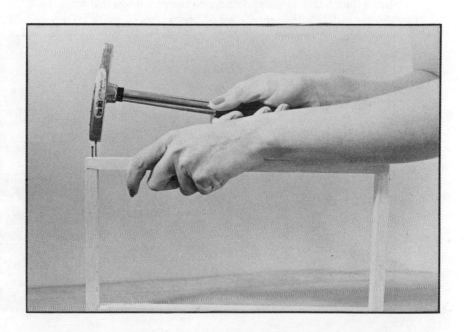

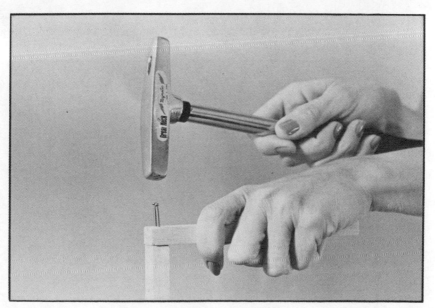

3.   For the base of the diorama, cut a piece of string a little longer than *half* the longest side of the diorama. For example, if the base is 12", then cut the string 7". Tie the string to a pencil. Measure the string again and place a thumb tack at the end opposite the pencil where it measures 6". Push the tack into the center edge of the cardboard, mark off a semicircle.

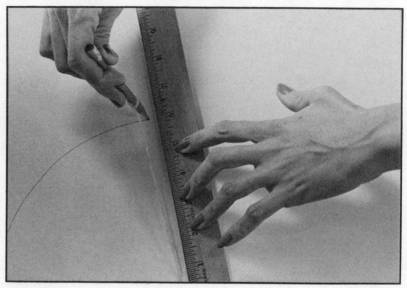

Take the X-ACTO® knife and cut out the semicircle. Be careful to place newspapers underneath the cardboard for padding to keep from cutting into the table.

4.   Once the base is cut, attach it to the frame base using thumb tacks. Place the tacks one inch apart so that the base is held secure by the frame.

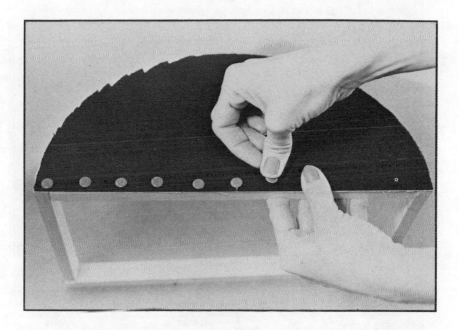

5.   Use a piece of string to measure the circumference of the semicircular base. Place the string along the longest base side of the mat board. Measure the height of the diorama with a ruler and mark off one side along the short edge of the mat board. Then make the same measurement marks on the inside of the mat board. Cut the mat board with the X-ACTO® knife, again with proper padding underneath (see page 156 for photographs).

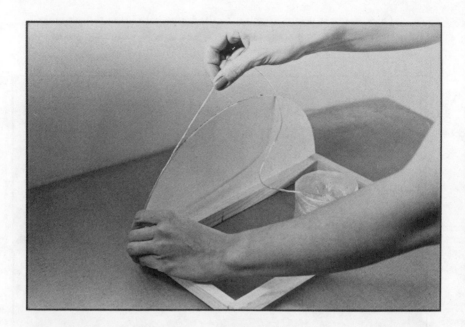

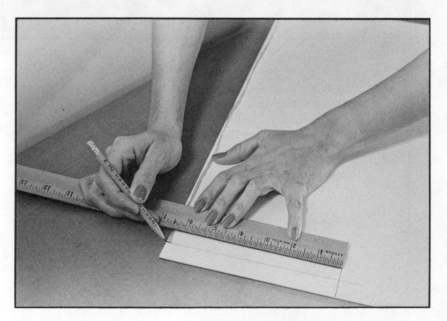

6. Attach the short sides of the mat board to the frame using thumb tacks approximately one inch apart. Place masking tape over the tacks along the sides and base and then around the semicircle to hold the back and base together.

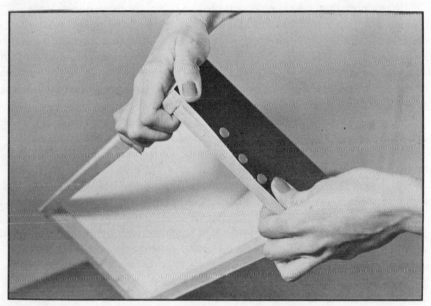

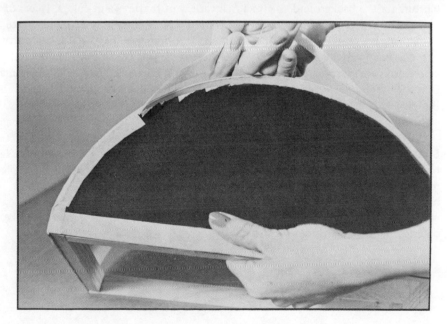

You now have the shell of the diorama. Some individuals prefer to sketch, draw, and paint the background directly onto the mat board *before* attaching it, while others draw the scene on a separate piece of paper and glue or tape it to the mat board. You will want to experiment with both methods.

Remember that a diorama is supposed to be a three-dimensional scene. If this is to be so, your students will have to try drawing or cutting out roads or mountains which are wider or larger when placed in the foreground and smaller in the background to give perspective to the diorama. Also, remind them when painting a sky to use a darker blue or darker colors for the horizon and lighter colors toward the top of the skyline. Also, dark colors are best for the sides of the diorama and lighter colors should be used for the foreground.

Using a variety of different size objects, animals or people in the diorama is best. For example, smaller animals should be placed closer to the background, while the larger animals should be placed in the foreground. Every possible means should be used to give depth and perspective.

If light is needed to illuminate the scene, it is best to keep it out of the sight of the viewer. A sign at the top of the diorama naming what the scene depicts is an excellent cover for lighting. A small flashlight or small wattage bulb attached to an electric cord placed directly behind the sign might provide just enough light. Always be careful that the bulb is not placed directly against the diorama to avoid the possibility of a fire.

Many techniques can be used to color and/or decorate the diorama. Tempra or water colors, large felt-tip pens, or sponges dipped in a watercolored glue-sand mixture for the background all give a rich variety of textures and colors. Pieces of material or newspaper strips dipped in a watery glue mixture may be molded into mountains, laid into place, and then painted. Tree branches may be stuck in putty or a pine cone may be painted green to represent a bush. Lakes and streams could be created with clear glass over blue cellophane or with a small mirror. Flowers may be made by taping crepe paper to a stem or by folding tissues on a pipe cleaner. Buildings may be made with soap pieces, sugar cubes, popsicle sticks, small twigs or by simply folding and gluing cardboard together.

There are just as many ways to make animals and people as there are objects. Students will want to experiment with simple cut-out figures on cardboard with tabs to hold them in place, with carving their own from soap or wood, with wire, papier mâché or yarn figures and even with figures brought from their toy collection at home. They should be encouraged to try as many of these techniques as they are willing. With each new attempt using a different medium, their dioramas will take on a totally different effect for the viewer.

SAMPLE FORMAT FOR MAKING A DIORAMA

The activity given below began with the teacher sharing a picture book with first grade students. Notice the way in which the teacher has documented the sharing experience with complete bibliographic information on the book, an introductory activity, the story outline, and follow-up activities, one of which includes making a diorama.

■ ■ ■

Barrett, Judi. *Animals Should Definitely Not Wear Clothing.* Illustrated by Ron Barrett. New York: Atheneum Press, 1970.

GRADE LEVELS:	K–2
INTRODUCTORY ACTIVITY:	I would provide at least 2 or 3 small stuffed animals wearing clothing pieces of some sort, introduce them, and lead into a discussion of animals as pets and friends. Then, asking the children about their pets and if they ever wore clothes, I would lead into the book.
STORY:	Through humorous pictures, the idea is presented about why animals should definitely not wear clothing. Pictures include a porcupine, camel, snake, mouse, sheep, pig, hen, kangaroo, giraffe, goat, walrus, moose, opossums, and an elephant.
FOLLOW-UP ACTIVITIES:	I would ask various children if they could think of any other reasons why animals should not wear clothing. This could lead into either drawing time or else into acting out some of the animals and their problems. The song "Talk to the Animals" from the motion picture *Dr. Doolittle* could be worked in here.
	Each child could also select an animal and with the teacher's help make a small diorama appropriate for that animal. Children would draw the animal on construction paper, paste it onto cardboard and then cut it out. Tabs could be glued to the bottom of the animal to make it stand up. Doll clothes could be taken from a book to see if any of the clothing really looked right on the animals.

–George Stewart

ANNOTATED BIBLIOGRAPHY

Brown, James W., Richard B. Lewis, and Fred F. Harcleroad. *A V Instruction: Technology, Media, and Methods.* 5th ed. New York: McGraw-Hill, 1977, p. 279.
The authors describe various ways to make dioramas more effective and realistic to the viewer. Illustrated.

Currie, Dorothy H. *Making Dioramas and Displays.* Dansville, NY: F. A. Owen Publishing Co., 1965.
Describes in detail how to construct a variety of dioramas, scenes and displays. How to make the properties to be used in creating realistic, yet inexpensive, dioramas are also discussed. Illustrated.

"Dioramas," *Britannica Junior Encyclopaedia.* Vol. 5. Chicago: Encyclopaedia Britannica, Inc., 1973, pp. 108-110.
Provides a definition of the term and the step-by-step procedures involved in preparing and making a diorama. Illustrated.

How to Make and Use a Diorama. 16mm film, color, 20 min. McGraw-Hill, 1956.
Shows how to construct effective miniature scenes with students. Also provides information on basic materials and techniques.

Wittich, Walter S., and Charles F. Schuller. *Instructional Technology: Its Nature and Use.* 5th ed. New York: Harper and Row, 1973, pp. 167-69.
The authors define the term and provide examples of ways dioramas may be used to enhance instruction. Illustrated.

SUGGESTIONS FOR FOLLOW-UP ACTIVITIES

Only one type of diorama—the traditional—was explored in depth. You might want to construct one of the other types as shown on pages 147-149. I have encouraged students when we jointly completed working on the traditional type to select one of the others and build it at home. Instead of making an entire sequence of ten or twelve that have been storyboarded, they may want to select a short poem or a scene from nature to realistically portray in a box or flat-figure diorama.

Making dioramas naturally leads into the construction of similar methods of illustrating an idea or story. Students may want to read a play or short story or research a particular topic for a report and illustrate their idea not only with a written report but also with a scene. Scenes may vary in size as well as in structure. A student may wish to display a panorama encompassing a scene of buildings, roadways, mountains and trees, or he may elect to simply cut out hand-drawn figures with tab bottoms such as animals and trees and glue these onto the base of the scene.

If all students are working on a research assignment that covers similar items yet in some way distinct—for example, costumes of a particular group of countries or animals that live in the water—a display might be appropriate. Dorothy Currie in *Making Dioramas and Displays* (1965) defines the display as "an exhibit of related objects arranged in a pleasing manner" (p. 36). Displays may be arranged in such a way to show the development or sequence of events in history, or they may simply depict how similar items may be made in a variety of ways. Displays may be placed on tables or in locked cabinets for viewing. I have set up many a display in book cases in the media center in an area where children would have a difficult time reaching a book but where a display may be adequately viewed but not touched.

SUPPLIERS OF EQUIPMENT AND SOFTWARE

You should experience no difficulty whatsoever in locating the necessary equipment from your local hardware and/or discount stores and the software from your arts supply dealer. Careful shopping by phone *first* using the specification under "Summary List of Estimated Costs" will not only save you time but will also cut down on unnecessary expenditures.

BIBLIOGRAPHY

Anderson, Bert. "Cameraless Animation: How It Can Turn Kids On," *Film Library Quarterly* (Winter 1972-73):27-30.

Anderson, Chuck. *The Electric Journalist: An Introduction to Video.* New York: Praeger Publishers, 1973.

The Basics of Cinematography (1977). Eastman Kodak Company, Department 454, Rochester, NY 14650.

Boniol, John D. "Making Slides Without Cameras," *School Library Journal* (April 1975):36.

Brown, James W., and Richard B. Lewis, Eds. *AV Instructional Technology Manual for Independent Study.* 5th ed. New York: McGraw-Hill, 1977.

Brown, James W., Richard B. Lewis, and Fred F. Harcleroad. *AV Instruction: Technology, Media, and Methods.* 5th ed. New York: McGraw-Hill, 1977.

Brown, Robert M. *Educational Media: A Competency Approach.* Columbus, OH: Charles E. Merrill, 1973.

Brown, Richard. "Exciting? Dramatic? Filmstrips?" *Film Library Quarterly* (Spring 1970):19-22.

Cheharbakhshi, Henry, producer. *A Film about Filmmaking, Making a Sound Film, A Film about Film Editing,* and *A Film about Cinematography.* International Film Bureau, Inc., 332 South Michigan Avenue, Chicago, IL 60604.

Cloke, William. "Filmstrips—How to Make Your Own," *California School Libraries* (Winter 1976):15-18.

Currie, Dorothy H. *Making Dioramas and Displays.* Dansville, NY: F. A. Owen Publishing Co., 1965.

"Dioramas," *Britannica Junior Encyclopaedia.* Vol. 5. Chicago: Encyclopaedia Britannica, Inc., 1973, pp. 108-110.

The Electronic Rainbow: Television. 16mm, color, 23 min. Pyramid Films, Box 1048, Santa Monica, CA 90406, 1977. $325 sale, $35 rental.

Fiddle-de-dee. 16mm, color, 4 min. Distributed by International Film Bureau, Inc., 332 South Michigan Avenue, Chicago, IL 60604, 1947. $65 sale, $6 rental.

Filmmaking Fundamentals. 16mm, color, 20 min. Brown-Collen Productions, 1972. $275 sale, $20 rental.

Films and Fun. 8 color sound filmstrips, 8 cassettes. AIMS Instructional Media Services, Inc., 626 Justin Avenue, Glendale, CA 91201. $160 series, $20 each part.

101 Great Filmmaking Tips. Editors of *Super8Filmmaker*, P.O. Box 10052, Dept. H1004, Palo Alto, CA 94303.

Harwood, D. *Everything You Always Wanted to Know about Video Tape Recording.* 2nd ed. Queens, NY: VTR Publishing Co., 1975.

Hatch, Lawrence A. "Making and Testing a Filmstrip," *California School Libraries* (Spring 1973):6-9.

Hobson, Andrew, and Mark Hobson. *Film Animation as a Hobby.* New York: Sterling Publishing, 1975.

How to Animate a Gingerbread Boy. 16mm, color, 14 min. A Rainy Day Film. Churchill Films, 662 North Robertson Blvd., Los Angeles, CA 90069, 1973. $195 sale (including book).

How to Make and Use a Diorama. 16mm film, color, 20 min. New York: McGraw-Hill, 1956.

Kahn, Linda. "VTR in the Classroom—or—How I Learned to Stop Worrying and Start Saving Cardboard Boxes," *Media & Methods* (April 1975):40-41.

Kemp, Jerrold E. *Planning and Producing Audiovisual Materials.* 3rd ed. New York: Thomas Y. Crowell, 1975.

Matzkin, Myron A. *Super 8mm Movie Making Simplified.* Englewood Cliffs, NJ: Prentice-Hall, 1975.

McBride, Otis. "Local Production with 35mm Photography," *School Libraries* (Winter 1971):25-27.

Media Production Series. Media Systems, Inc., 3637 East 7800 South, Salt Lake City, UT 84121.

Minor, Ed, and Harvey R. Frye. *Techniques for Producing Visual Instructional Media.* New York: McGraw-Hill, 1970.

Mohr, Nelda, and Thalia-Mann Tissot. "Cents and Non-Cents of AV Crafts," *Top of the News* (Jan. 1972):173-78.

Movies with a Purpose. Eastman Kodak Company, 1187 Ridge Road West, Rochester, NY 14650. Free.

Neighbors. 16mm, color, 9 min. National Film Board of Canada. Distributed by International Film Bureau, Inc., 332 South Michigan Avenue, Chicago, IL 60604, 1952. $135 sale, $10 rental.

Orgren, Carl F. "Production of Slide-Tape Programs," *Unabashed Librarian* (Summer 1975):25-28.

Palmer, Millicent. "Creating Slide-Tape Library Instruction: The Librarian's Role," *Drexel Library Quarterly* (July 1972):251-67.

Ray, Mary L. "Videotaping: You and Your Kids Can Do It," *Teacher* (Jan. 1975): 47-48, 106.

Robinson, Richard. *The Video Primer.* New York: Links Book Publishers, 1974.

Robson, Walt. "Getting Your Bait Back," *Video Systems* (March 1977):44-46.

Rosenberg, Kenyon C., and John S. Doskey. *Media Equipment: A Guide and Dictionary.* Littleton, CO: Libraries Unlimited, 1976.

Ryan, Mack. "Preparing a Slide-Tape Program: A Step-by-Step Approach; Part I/ Part II," *Audiovisual Instruction* (Sept. 1975/Nov. 1975): 36-38/36-38.

Ryan, Steve S. "Teaching Film," *Audiovisual Instruction* (Sept. 1977):38-39.

Sights, Karen. "Animation . . . Pixilation . . . Creation for Kids," *Media Spectrum* (1976):29-30, 32.

Taylor, Charles B. "To Videotape or Not to Videotape," *Audiovisual Instruction* (Jan. 1977):33-34, 39-40.

Tucker, Nancy J. "What You Always Wanted to Know about VTR: Once Over Lightly," *Media Spectrum* (1974):14-15, 23.

Turner, Philip M. *Handbook for In-School Media Personnel.* Green Bay, WI: PLT Publications, 1975.

Vitz, Carol. "Recipe for a Filmstrip," *California School Libraries* (Spring 1976): 19-26.

Wagner, Betty J., and E. Arthur Stunard. *Making and Using Inexpensive Classroom Media.* Palo Alto, CA: Education Today Co., 1975.

Winslow, Ken, ed. *Video Play Program Source Guide.* Ridgefield, CT: C.S. Tepfer Publishing Co., 1974.

Wittich, Walter S., and Charles F. Schuller. *Instructional Technology: Its Nature and Use.* 5th ed. New York: Harper and Row, 1973.

Yulsman, Jerry. *The Complete Book of 8mm (Super-8, Single-8, Standard-8) Movie-making.* New York: Coward, McCann, and Geoghegan, 1972.

INDEX